CLIMBING BACK

A Family's Journey through Brain Injury

Elise Rosenhaupt

Peninsula Road Press
San Francisco

Library of Congress Cataloguing-in-Publication Data
    Rosenhaupt, Elise, 1948—
    Climbing back : a family's journey through brain injury / written by Elise Rosenhaupt; foreword by Joseph Ratner.—1ˢᵗ ed.
        p. cm.
    Includes bibliographical references.
    ISBN 978-0-9836980-2-9 (pbk.)
    1. Brain—Wounds and injuries. 2. Brain—Wounds and injuries—Rehabilitation. 3. Brain—Wounds and injuries—Patients—United States—Biography. 4. Brain—Wounds and injuries—Patients—United States—Families. I. Rosenhaupt, Elise. II. Ratner, Joseph. III. Title. IV. Title: A family's journey through brain injury.

RC387.5.F67 C75 2015

362.1'97—dc23

2015943019

First edition, June 2015

Published by:
Peninsula Road Press
San Francisco, California
www.peninsularoad.com

Order additional copies at www.spdbooks.com.
Contact the author at ClimbingBackER@gmail.com.

ISBN: 978-0-9836980-2-9

Interior design and production © by Richard Mahler at Relham LLC, www.relham.com. Printed in the USA by McNaughton & Gunn, Saline, MI.

For My Family

CONTENTS

FOREWORD

TRAUMATIC BRAIN INJURY is always a life-altering event, both for the person who suffers it, and for the family and loved ones who must endure the painful course of recovery and the often distressing sequelae of an injured brain. The very phrase is frightening. As a psychiatrist with thirty years' experience working on a brain injury unit of a major rehabilitation hospital, I have had the privilege of working with patients and their families as they struggle to cope with, and try to comprehend the meaning of seeing themselves or their loved one in such a profoundly altered state. I am often struck by how little experience people have with head injury. It is as if those who suffer it live in a hidden part of our culture, often keeping to themselves, or worse, shunned by the general public. This, in spite of the fact that traumatic brain injury is common. The Center for Disease Control statistics tell us that there are 1.7 million reported instances of traumatic brain injury each year (and probably untold millions more unreported). And it is sad to experience the virtual epidemic of brain injury cases that have returned with our troops from Iraq and Afghanistan. And there is additional distress in learning of the large number of children and athletes with potentially permanent brain damage from head injuries and concussions while playing football and other sports.

There is a robust technical literature on brain injury, with several journals dedicated to various aspects of the diagnosis and treatment of this condition. There is one voice, however, that is largely missing, and that is the voice of the person and the family who are actually experiencing it. Now, Elise Rosenhaupt has given us that voice. In a memoir that is both profound and thorough, she somehow found the courage and the discipline to look this event straight in its horrible eye, and to take notes. The result is *Climbing Back*, the record of her son's brain injury and its unfolding as it affected his life and the life of his family.

Elise captures vividly the sense of shock and anxiety and confusion that arrives with that phone call every parent unconsciously fears receiving. "Your son has been struck by a car. He's in the hospital. We don't know how bad it is." Thus begins a journey no one would ever choose, but one which this young man, and his family, managed to finally engage on their own terms, with grace and dignity, and ultimately with a sense of victory. How they do it will be compelling reading for any professional in the field, and especially for those enduring the injury itself. And along the way, we learn truly invaluable clues and lessons about how to navigate through the complexities and ambiguities of a family's recovery.

We learn, for instance, the importance of having to rely on many experts, who suddenly have control of your child's body. We learn the more profound lesson of coming to rely on the family's own perception and judgment. A healthy disrespect for authority-for-its-own-sake becomes a path for the family, and for their son to slowly regain a sense of independence. Autonomy becomes a healing force on its own.

We learn the importance of not allowing the family to become isolated and enclosed. "It is as if we all arrive deaf and blind, in a trance, completely alone. Then the clouds begin to lift, we see one another, and eventually we speak." And we hear the even more important lesson of not becoming internally isolated. The fear, the tears, the anger must all be validated, must all be given their time to speak and be felt and shared.

As Martin moves through recovery, he begins the healthy process of separating from his mother, who describes her watchful nurturing of his early recovery as "a speeded up replay of motherhood." As her process of healing continues, she makes a journey back to the sites of the trauma, the ICU, the acute care hospital, the rehabilitation facility. She tells us with great wisdom, "To be in all those places with those same people, and to have Martin well, in some way undid the spell of my sorrow." She concludes, "Knowing that nothing can keep us safe, how do we live? . . . I watch Martin in the way he has of being absolutely present in his joy at being with those he loves, and I feel as though, knowing that nothing can keep any of us safe, he knows how to live." And now, having read this remarkable document, perhaps we will know better how to live as well.

Joseph S. Ratner, M.D.
Chief of Psychiatry, New England Rehabilitation Hospital

Author's Note: The names of some people in this book have been changed.

The World Turned Upside Down:
New York and Massachusetts

People give themselves away as they cross streets.

Hans Rosenhaupt [Martin's grandfather]
penciled on a scrap of paper found years after his death.

THE LAST TIME I saw our son before his injury, my husband and I were walking toward Harvard Square. The three of us had eaten supper together. I turned to watch Martin cross the traffic-busy street, heading back toward Lowell House and his room. His navy pants hung loose about his tall frame. The wet streets shone with rain. A few steps farther on I turned again, and he had disappeared.

Always I am alert to disaster that might strike. Knowing this could be the last time I see someone, I lock their images in my brain— my husband, Tom, waving as he drives off to Utah, his car full with camping gear; Sarah, our daughter, turning as she vanishes down the airport corridor; my mother, looking from her doorway as I cross the courtyard and head home.

IT IS EARLY morning in New York, Wednesday, October 21st, 1998. Sarah and I are still half asleep on her futon when Tom answers our daughter's phone.

"Where is Martin now? What did the surgeon say?"

Something is terribly wrong. The room has run out of air.

For long stretches between his few questions, Tom is silent.

He says we will be there in a few hours, and hangs up.

Martin—our son, Sarah's brother—is in Massachusetts General Hospital. They have operated on his brain.

"Shall I come with you?" Sarah asks.

"No," I say, and Tom says, "Stay here in New York. We'll call you. You can come on the train after we see how he is."

Not taking Sarah with us is a choice I wish I could undo. I am not thinking clearly, only wanting to keep her safe. Do Tom and I imagine we cannot care for her while we are saving Martin? Will this be a trip to say farewell?

Still, our twenty-two-year-old daughter accepts our decree as if she were still a child.

BETWEEN NEW YORK and Boston in our car, we realize we could have flown. We could be there now. Will we get there in time?

Tom drives, and I call our home in Santa Fe. Doctors have been calling all night and no one was home. Only in the morning has someone found, on a paper in Martin's wallet, his sister's phone number and reached us in New York.

On the answering machine, doctors ask, "Does Martin have a history of heart problems?"

I reach one doctor and tell him, "No problems—his heart is good."

He says something else but I don't understand what he is telling me. I only want to get to Martin.

At a gas station I buy coffee and doughnuts while Tom fills the tank. Back in the car we, who never run out of things to talk about, notice, or wonder at, are quiet.

The sun is bright. Trees are red and gold. I sip my sweet strong coffee. Will anything ever taste so good again?

Time doesn't move. We are in a car, between our daughter and our son, knowing only that we don't know what will happen. Soon we will know too much.

WE REACH BOSTON just past noon. The hospital is its own city within the city. Below towers of metal and concrete and glass, ambulances load and unload, taxis come and go, and gowned patients smoke cigarettes beside their IV stands. We run through continuously revolving doors, pass people hurrying through crowded hallways, go by ATM alcoves and coffee bars, and find the elevators.

On the tenth floor, a woman unlocks the Neurological Intensive Care door. She leads us to Martin—bandaged, bloody, unconscious. Tubes and wires run everywhere. At the center of the tangle lies our child. We touch him, we speak to him, we stay with him. We don't cry. We must be with him, nothing else.

What if we lose him?

We ask no questions when Oliver, his nurse, says we must leave the room. Oliver's efficiency and constant motion, along with the equipment in the room itself, tell us that Martin is in crisis. Experts know what to do. We must not get in their way.

A Little Help

"With a Little Help from My Friends"

The Beatles, Song Title

SENT OUT OF Martin's room, we sit in the waiting room outside the locked Neurological ICU. door. A small, fair-haired young man, wearing a tweed jacket and carrying a dark green book bag, stops in the hallway. I watch him as from a great distance. When he sees us, he knows right away who we are. Does he recognize Tom from his brown eyes and dark hair, like Martin's, from his trim build, his lean features, his hiking boots, all like Martin's? Does he spot me as Martin's mother? Or is it that Tom and I are so clearly there together, companions in a stunned silence?

Gene McAfee's title is Senior Tutor at Harvard's Lowell House. Martin has lived in Lowell since September, where we presumed he would be based for the next three years. Harvard's dozen undergraduate houses are more than just living quarters—each has its own dining hall, libraries, teams, drama groups, and traditions. Designed to create a sense of community in the often intimidating university, each house has a presiding master and administrators, as well as associated graduate students, faculty, and university officials.

Gene McAfee came to the hospital with Diana Eck, Master of Lowell House, last night while Martin was in surgery. Beyond that, he has nothing more to tell and just sits with us, waiting.

Time doesn't pass and it doesn't stand still. It is as if we have been lifted out of time to where we simply *are*, and to where Martin simply *is*. Something will happen, but not now, not yet.

Diana Eck arrives. She is tall, with fading blond hair cut to just above her shoulders, serious without the frumpiness of so many Cambridge women. She is a professor of comparative religion and Indian studies. Her partner, and co-master of Lowell House, Dorothy Austin, is an Episcopal priest who spends several days each week in New Jersey teaching psychology and religion.

When, last summer, Harvard wrote that they had chosen two women as the new masters of Lowell House, Tom said the university was making a mistake. His own Harvard House master had been an old-fashioned gentleman scholar who proffered wisdom with port after dinner. For Tom, eleven when his own father died, Master Finley represented a fatherly ideal. He doubted that two women could provide the atmosphere he had so valued.

TOM AND I met in my college dining hall, thirty years ago. He still claims he'd come for supper only because the food at Radcliffe, where Harvard's women students lived before the university's housing became coed, was better than Harvard's food, but I don't believe him. He showed up, some days later, to offer me a motorcycle ride. What I remember is the extra helmet he brought for me. He wanted to keep me safe.

We've been married twenty-five years. I'm not an easy wife. I cry easily, get angry fast, and foresee disaster long before he does. I don't know whether the calmness he offers after my tempests means he's forgiven me or just that he's untroubled by my tears. But his calm is what I need, a gift.

Years ago, when he was starting as a real estate broker, he would tell me about someone who was "impossible, unreasonable, an idiot." When he picked up the phone, I anticipated thunder. But then I heard him politely explain his thinking, often suggesting, "Put yourself in my client's position."

When Tom blusters, sometimes I forget it's just noise. We show each other our harsher parts, parts we struggle to control so we can be the better people we want to be.

He expected Diana to fall short as a house master. Minutes after she arrives, she and Tom are walking in the hallway, their arms around one another.

MARTIN'S FRIENDS COME to the hospital—his roommate Dave, Ultimate Frisbee teammates, and Rachel. Rachel might have been Martin's girlfriend last spring—we don't know, because Martin is so private. Last night they all waited in the emergency room with Gene and Diana. Hours later, when there was no news and no hope for news, Diana brought them home to her Lowell House kitchen and made cocoa. They stand with us in the waiting room.

"Martin is strong," one of the young men says.

"He's an incredible man," says another.

"He's going to be all right."

We put our arms around one another in a circle, silent.

Paying Attention:
Massachusetts General Hospital

. . . Why weave fantasies when reality is so fascinating and
challenging? Truth is both stranger and more important than
fiction.

Francis D. Moore, M.D., "Ethics at Both Ends of Life"

IN THE EVENING, Martin's nurse is Annie. Like Oliver, Annie has only Martin to care for. We take care to anticipate her moves and stay out of her way. We hear that ICU rules limit the time we are allowed to be in Martin's small room, but Annie does not ask us to leave. Does she think this may be our last time with him?

I sit by Martin's bed all night, my hand touching his arm. A breathing tube is taped to his mouth. Another tube drains fluid from his brain into a calibrated receptacle. An IV drips a sedative into him. Last night, before we got the phone call at Sarah's, a neurosurgeon opened his skull to perform a ventriculostomy, draining fluid off his swelling brain, relieving the intracranial pressure. Without that relief, the swelling and the accumulating fluid would compress the brain and constrict the flow of blood. Martin's brain would be further injured.

ON THURSDAY MORNING, Tom and Clint, a friend since college who still lives in Cambridge, go to where Martin was hit. Memorial Drive is a narrow four lane highway, shaded by sycamore trees. When we were in college, the city of Cambridge was getting ready to widen Memorial Drive. Students started a movement to Save the Sycamores. They made signs, marched in protest, and wrote letters. The road did not get widened. It stayed narrow, shaded by sycamore trees. I think, *Perhaps cars now drive more slowly there than if the city had widened Memorial Drive. Perhaps the narrow road saved Martin's life.*

Unlike Tom, who wants to make logical sense of anything he can, I often look for small miracles. Perhaps that is my coping mechanism, my way of defying life's uncertainty.

Tom and Clint examine the skid marks, the chalk lines, and, Tom says, the blood on the street. I ask him not to tell me any more of what they saw. He telephones a witness who was driving in the other direction when the car hit Martin. The man did not see Martin walking across Memorial Drive, but he did see the car that hit him. He says it wasn't speeding.

The accident happened late at night. There was no moon. Martin was wearing dark clothes.

Clint has represented accident victims for years. Had there been any chance that the driver was at fault, he would have cautioned us about what we should or shouldn't say or do. Because he and Tom are certain the accident wasn't the driver's fault, we do not need to monitor ourselves. We can concentrate wholly on helping Martin recover.

WHENEVER THEY CHANGE IVs, or wash him, or take him somewhere for CT scans and x-rays, whenever there is a nursing shift change, and whenever the doctors come by, the nurse sends us out. We do not challenge our banishment; Martin's survival is at stake.

Still, there is no other place for us. He is my center, the image I see when I shut my eyes and, no matter what is in front of me, when my eyes are open. He is a constant presence when we are with his friends, with Gene and Diana, when we are calling Sarah, and when we eat whatever food someone brings. I go to the bathroom fast so I will not miss a moment. There is nothing in my world but wanting Martin to live.

DR. PECHET FINDS us in the waiting room on Thursday afternoon. A retired endocrinologist associated with Lowell House, Pechet has marched into the ICU to see Martin. "There seems to be no paralysis," he says, "and Martin is young and strong." Although he is not Martin's doctor, we are grateful for his assurances. Dr. Pechet and another Lowell House affiliate, a medical student who went to Harvard College, sit in the waiting room with us. They try to answer our questions and offer to help. We cannot imagine what they can do.

That evening, one nurse tells us that Martin, when he arrived at Mass General, was *unresponsive*. We do not know if she means he was in a coma. As the days go by, we learn that even the doctors do not agree on whether our son is, or ever was, in a coma.

> *Stupor* is a state in which the patient is unresponsive but can be aroused briefly by a strong stimulus, such as sharp pain. *Coma* is a state in which the patient is

totally unconscious, unresponsive, unaware, and unarousable. Patients in a coma do not respond to external stimuli, such as pain or light, and do not have sleep-wake cycles. [*"Hope Through Research," National Institute of Neurological Disorders and Stroke pamphlet.*]

Among those who say Martin is, or was, in a coma, there is no consensus as to where he is, or where he was, on the *coma scale* that assesses responsiveness. One doctor says Martin at first was *un*responsive; another says he was *barely* responsive. One doctor says he is coming *out* of his coma, and another says he has never been *in* a coma.

But because current medical wisdom says a badly injured brain needs protection from potentially damaging agitation and seizures, Martin is kept sedated, intentionally unconscious. Still, I never doubt that he knows we are beside him, hears our voices, and feels the touch of our hands. But I do not know if he can make the journey back to us.

Tom and I stand beside Martin and tell him we are there to take care of him. We move quickly out of every nurse's way. We must be absolutely present so Martin will hear our voices and feel our hands on him. The nurses tell us both to go to our friend's house and sleep, but we will not leave Martin alone. Later, Tom says that he does not know whether our being there, with our voices and our hands touching him and the prayers we make, influenced Martin's recovery. But when I ask him, "Would you want all those things for yourself?" he says, "Yes."

There is no space for us to ask why this has happened, or what will happen next.

We never talk about what we fear most.

We don't fall apart. We are holding our breath.

OUR MINDS WHIRL to track what is happening. We are trying to fit together pieces of a jigsaw puzzle, not knowing what the finished picture will be.

Doctors are working to figure out what is serious and what is not.

Because of the abrasions on Martin's legs, orthopedic specialists look for fractures. X-rays show no breaks there.

Martin's heart alarmed the doctors when he was first brought to Mass General. From the questions several doctors left on our answering machine, I guess that his heart's rhythms were all wrong. Did they have to re-start his heart? I don't ask. After a few days, we meet the cardiologist in the elevator. He tells us he has signed off on Martin's case. Our son's heart, at least, has weathered the trauma.

X-rays do show five fractures of Martin's left scapula—his shoulder blade. An orthopedist says the pieces are all in the right place. They will heal without medical intervention.

When the car hit Martin it sent him flying over a hundred feet. He landed on his head in the road. At the scene, his movements indicated to the paramedics that he had severe brain injury. Their first attempt to put a tube down his throat, so they could pump air into his lungs, failed. Their second try succeeded.

The paramedics then made a decision that may have saved Martin's life. They took him not to Mount Auburn, the closest hospital, and not to Cambridge City Hospital, also close. Tom thinks the light late night traffic helped them decide to drive the extra few miles to Massachusetts General, one of the world's great hospitals.

I am not interested in why the ambulance took Martin to Mass General, but I see that, for Tom, figuring such things out is important.

13

When so little makes sense, he wants to make sense of anything he can. It's his way to defy the randomness of life.

WHEN WE ARRIVED at Mass General, half a day after the accident, one doctor said the first *twenty-four hours* were critical. A day later, another doctor tells us the first *three days* are critical. A day after that, another speaks of the critical *first five* days. Trying to make sense of what is happening, we understand only that we are powerless.

What damage has been done the doctors cannot tell us. Which functions will come back they do not know. Again and again, we hear the same message, from doctors and from nurses—every brain trauma story is different. With traumatic brain injury, no one can predict what will happen.

Tom and I compare what we've heard from the medical experts. We try to remember who each is—orthopedist or trauma specialist; the nurse on duty when Martin was brought, after his surgery, to the neurological ICU in the middle of the night, or the one who took over in the morning; intern or resident or veteran doctor. We try to understand: *How long is critical?* and *What are the immediate dangers?*

When the sedative lowers Martin into a deep sleep, protecting him from the mental and physical agitation that usually accompany traumatic brain injury, a ventilator and ET (endotracheal) tube keep him breathing.

One nurse likens being on a ventilator to breathing under water through a straw. She says it is what she most dreads for herself.

The systems helping Martin survive are interconnected: sedation helps relieve the pressure in his brain and also depresses his breathing. We want him to be set free from the machinery that breathes for him, from the IV that sedates him, and from the tube that drains fluid from his brain.

At times, Tom and I talk about the green numbers on the monitors. They record Martin's heartbeats, blood pressure, respiration rate, degree of oxygen saturation in his blood, sedative level, and intracranial pressure. We note changes in the numbers and hold onto them as signposts that might guide us to safety. We do not speak our fears.

Just once, I think, *It is possible they will ask us about organ donation.* Five years ago, when I went with Martin to get his driver's license, neither of us hesitated at the question on the form. At fifteen (New Mexico, a state only since 1912, licenses drivers that young), he signed up to be a donor. Perhaps because I know what his answer would be, I think only fleetingly that someone may ask that question.

We cannot imagine how Martin will recover enough to leave the ICU.

Deep Down

Open your eyes
To the good blackness not of your room alone
But of the sky you trust is over it . . . .

Richard Wilbur, "Walking to Sleep"

I OFTEN DRIFT AWAY. My imaginings distract me from what's in front of me. Once, in Santa Fe, where houses come in fifty shades of brown, I pointed out one that had just been painted blue. Tom said it had been blue for years.

Now I am paying close attention, noticing everything—the richness of my coffee, how Tom and Diana hold onto each other in the hallway, where the nurse is headed, and where I need to move to stay out of the way.

How I interpret what I observe is sometimes odd. One detail particularly puzzles me—a tape securing an IV to Martin's arm is inscribed with his sister's birthdate, 12/01. When I show it to Tom, he tells me I am looking at the writing upside down and shows me that the tape actually reads 10/21, the date the nurse started the IV.

There are no long empty hours, as I might have foreseen. Being present takes all my strength and every minute is full.

WE COUNT TIME in pieces of days. Almost midnight on Wednesday is one day from the accident. Dawn is the next destination. Out the north-facing window of Martin's room, we see planes taking off from Boston's airport. Every day is warm and clear. By the second midnight, two days have passed. Another dawn comes. We touch Martin and we speak to him. Planes rise silently in the distance.

Every two hours, the nurses send us out of Martin's room before they interrupt the sedative, propofol, so they can assess his responsiveness. On Friday, the third day, his nurse lets us stay when she turns off the sedative. Martin rises to the surface, opens his eyes, and looks straight at us. He closes his eyes.

The nurse asks him to move a finger, make a fist, do thumbs up, wiggle his toes, right, left. No response. Then she shouts her commands at him, trying to reach him through the sedative's fog. We watch his right index finger move, but nothing else. To check his reflexes, she scrapes his feet. She pinches him, twists his flesh. Eventually, he moves one left finger a tiny bit.

We are jubilant. A day later, Martin moves his toes, just on the right side. He has red bruises from days of pinches and twists. Tom says, "The fact that he reacted is such a relief. I'm not so concerned that they beat the shit out of him." Making a connection to his injured brain is what matters. Bruises will heal.

Only much later does Tom tell me he has imagined Martin living out his life in a wheelchair, his left side paralyzed. I do not think anything beyond hoping he will wiggle his toes. It is almost a week after the accident before his left foot responds with a tiny movement.

TOM DOES NOT easily talk about his feelings. He translates his emotions into needs and channels his energy into meeting those needs. I have to push him to talk about any problems. He just wants to solve them.

He remembers what he felt while Martin lay unconscious in the ICU: "More than anything, you want him to come up from the sedative. What we wanted most was to see if he was going to be Martin, and hoped for a few more minutes before they put him under again. When he came out, he had so much pain—you realized that the sedative was what he needed, that he was just so hurt. I found myself saying, 'Okay, okay.' It was like crying uncle—let him go under. The answer to his getting better was that he had to go down."

When the sedative is turned off and Martin becomes conscious, he works his mouth trying to dislodge the ET tube's mouthpiece. He can't talk and his eyes are full of frustration and pain. We tell him, "We are taking care of you, and the tube is helping you breathe. You will be all right."

Then the nurse turns on the sedative and Martin loses consciousness. He is so deeply unconscious that, without the ventilator and ET tube sending air into his lungs, he would not be breathing.

We want them to take Martin off the sedative so they can take out his ET tube. Afterward, Tom says, "That was my biggest goal, getting the goddamn breathing tube out. It was just agony. Martin was waking up enough that you could tell that thing was killing him."

On Friday, after he moves his finger for the nurse, I ask

Martin to blink if he can hear us.

He blinks once.

I sensed that he heard us, and I believed that he saw us and felt us touching him, and now this simple blink affirms our hope that he will make the journey back.

Then Martin cries out in pain and his nurse turns the sedative back on. Tom and I watch our child go down, as if he is slipping under water, to where we cannot reach him. We watch the green numbers that tell how much propofol the IV is dripping into him.

It is as if by knowing how deep down he has gone, by knowing where he has gone, we can stay connected to him. We wait for someone to turn the sedative off the next time, so Martin can climb to the surface once again.

WHILE WE ARE out of his room, nursing aides care for Martin in ways we slowly discover. We learn that the lollipop-looking green sponges on sticks are saturated with mouthwash, and that the aides clean Martin's teeth and gums with them. They wash his hair and shave him. They trim his fingernails. I think of my childhood book, *Beauty and the Beast*, where invisible magic hands pour the wine and serve the feast and each night turn the covers back on Beauty's bed.

The nurses keep urging us to go our friend's home, to rest. They say Martin does not need us. They remind us that his nurse's only task is caring for him. They caution that, when Martin leaves Mass General, we, and he, will need all our strength. They do not predict when this will happen, but they warn that the next stage will be an incredibly long ordeal. We will have to help Martin recover, or, perhaps, learn to accept what parts of him will not get better.

At a practical level, the nurses are right. We need to be healthy. I have a bronchial infection that began in New York as a cold. I am terrified someone will say I can't be with Martin because I am sick. I breathe into handkerchiefs, and go out of the room when I have to cough.

But I will not leave Martin in Intensive Care without me or Tom there.

Tom is at Mass General most of the time. He sits with Martin, talks with doctors, finds the cafeteria, and brings food to share with me. In the morning, he goes to the coffee bar that we pass on the ground floor on our way to the elevators. He waits in a line so long it almost blocks the main corridor. He says he imagines that someone sent hundreds of Central Casting extras over to Mass General, directing them to walk back and forth in the corridors and ride up and down in the elevators.

In the afternoons, he stays with Martin and I go to Clint's house. Clint's buttoned-up ancestors watch from their portraits in his guestroom as I gather our clothes to put into the washing machine, climb into the narrow bed, and fall asleep. When the washing machine's clatter stops, I wake, move clothes to the dryer, and sleep again. I wake, fold the clothes, make scrambled eggs and toast, eat, walk ten minutes to Central Square, and take the subway back to Mass General.

LATE AT NIGHT, the nurse sends me out of Martin's room. She takes him somewhere many floors down for x-rays or CT scans. Alone in the waiting room, I figure out how to turn off the lights. I try to fall asleep sitting in a chair. Then I find that an armchair pulls out to make a flat hard bed. Another nurse brings me blankets and a pillow. She promises to wake me when Martin returns to the ICU.

Starting to fall asleep, I wake up, terrified.

"Martin will be well," I whisper as I shut my eyes again, "Martin will be well."

Being well may not mean getting better.

"Martin will be well." I whisper over and over.

I sleep.

The nurse wakes me when Martin comes back. In his room again, I hold Martin's hand and speak to him. I touch his cheek, his arms, his hands, his chest. I rub his feet. I never doubt that he feels me.

On Friday afternoon, the waiting room telephone rings. The driver whose car hit Martin has been trying to find us. He has barely slept. We wish we could tell him Martin will be all right, but all we can say is that we know it's not his fault.

SARAH WILL ARRIVE Friday evening, two and a half days after we left her in New York. We have talked with her every day, calling her at work, where she sits dazed, and calling her mornings and evenings at her apartment, where friends come to comfort and feed her. She lives in limbo, waiting to join us. We, too, are incomplete without her.

Diana Eck, the master of Lowell House, has arranged for Harvard Health Services' medical director to talk with us at the hospital Friday evening, at the same time Sarah's train is scheduled to arrive. I ask Diana if she can arrange for someone to meet our daughter at the station. She says she will meet Sarah herself.

ON FRIDAY EVENING, Christopher Coley comes to

the ICU waiting room. Tall, blond, and slender, he looks too young to be the director of Harvard's Health Services.

Dr. Coley asks what the neurosurgeon has told us, but, in the three days we have been at Mass General, we have not met the neurosurgeon. Coley looks startled—and offended. He says he will make sure that Dr. Hammer reports to us daily from now on.

He asks what the chief neurologist has said, and is upset that we have met only the neurology *resident*. Coley says he will ask the senior neurologist, who oversees the ICU, to talk with us every day.

A Less Traveled Path

I doubted if I should ever come back.

Robert Frost, *"The Road Not Taken"*

WE HAVE BEEN IGNORED by the doctors overseeing Martin's care. I wonder whether our looks play a part in this. We left Boston almost thirty years ago. I had grown up, never far from New York City, with European parents who loved London and knew Paris. Tom convinced me (I was in love, it was 1969, and I didn't need much convincing) to travel west with him after college.

We outfitted an old VW bus with an icebox and a mattress, and took off into the sunset. We parked at closed up summer homes along the Great Lakes, slept in cornfields, and watched ball lightning in the Badlands as rain lashed our bus. We wondered out loud whether the glowing balls of light were really Venusians. Dennis Hopper's spaced-out character, Billy, had laughed about the Venusians in *Easy Rider*, 1969's iconic film. High on LSD, we'd seen the movie just days before we hit the Badlands.

In Boulder, we stayed with Tom's freshman college roommate,

who dropped acid every morning just to see what would turn up. That was too extreme for us.

We drove south to Colorado Springs, where my parents lived before I was born, and where my father's mother lived until her death. My parents' old friends took us out to dinner. They loaned Tom a jacket and tie so the posh restaurant would let us in.

If we settled in Colorado Springs, we would always feel my parents' eyes on us.

We traveled south, stopping at communes along the way.

At Libre, the residents were artists with college degrees and money. They had rules that no one could build a cabin or dome within the view of anyone else's home.

At Drop City, an incoherent sailor and a young pregnant woman were pulling up the dome's oak floors and burning the wood to keep warm.

We stopped at New Buffalo, the classic commune we had glimpsed in *Easy Rider*. A toddler wearing only red rubber boots came out to greet us. After supper with the people living there, we went to bed in our tidy blue bus.

We drove down the Rio Grande valley in early October. The late day's sun shone through the yellow cottonwood leaves, and the sky was bluer than I had ever seen.

In a compound of five houses at the edge of Santa Fe, we rented a *casita*, a little house, for seventy-five dollars a month.

SANTA FE SUITED us. Two summers ago, Sarah's visiting college friend was surprised by the people at Tom's fiftieth birthday.

She said our friends—lawyer, carpenter, teacher, potter, exhibit builder, mortgage broker, and librarian—were nothing like her parents' circle of friends outside Philadelphia: all doctors. Santa Fe is diverse in other ways too, with families proud of ancestors who came from Spain hundreds of years ago, Native Americans, recent immigrants, poor people, rich people, and people, like us, just getting by.

Sarah embodies the Santa Fe modesty we like. When she graduated from high school, she had a red tassel on her cap because she was an honor student. When someone said, "I didn't know you were smart," she was amused. Few in her class knew she was headed for Columbia. Many had not heard of the Ivy League.

Neither Tom nor I is greatly changed from our college days. Tom still has lots of hair and neither of us is fat. Now, because of our hours outdoors in sunny Santa Fe, New Englanders often remark how healthy we look.

My hair is still long, still mostly dark, although the always escaping wisps around my face are turning white. A friend says I often look as if I've just come in from gardening. Sarah says that, like many women the world over, I have *hair*, not a *hairdo*.

Tom doesn't own a suit and my idea of proper dress is hardly Bostonian. I wear long skirts for comfort and warmth, and leather boots to keep my feet dry. In New Mexico, Tom looks preppy in the long-sleeved shirts he wears to keep the sun off, but in Boston his jeans and scuffed tennis shoes raise eyebrows. His impatience and curiosity take some people aback, and, although polite, he is never deferential.

WHATEVER THE REASON—our informal appearance

or the medical establishment's self-absorption—the senior doctors have not previously spoken with us. It doesn't seem fair that talking to doctors should be a privilege reserved for someone with the right connections. But too often it is.

After Dr. Coley's intervention, both the chief neurologist and the neurosurgeon talk with us every day. Dr. Hammer is British, tall, with ice blue eyes. He looks at the floor or above our heads while he speaks. Knowing that Hammer comes through the ICU at about six every morning, Tom is always there by five-thirty, ready with questions. He calls his conversations with the neurosurgeon, *Sixty Seconds at Six A.M.*

FEARING HER SHOCK when she sees Martin, I have tried to prepare Sarah on the phone. When Diana brings her to us on Friday evening, soon after Dr. Coley leaves, Sarah does not pause. She goes directly into the ICU. She touches her brother and speaks to him just as Tom and I do, knowing what he needs.

The nurse turns off the sedative. Martin rises into consciousness and looks at Sarah.

From my notebook:

> *The nurses know she is your sister by the eyelashes, so long, so black.*
> *She gives you her blue sleeve to feel, velvety chenille.*
> *You love the texture, eyes closed.*
> *She strips it off, down to her green tank top.*
> *Everyone looks at her.*
> *She looks at your hand learning chenille.*

SATURDAY, THE FOURTH night, Tom stays with Martin. Sarah and I sleep at Clint's. I wake several times and get up before dawn. I call a taxi and go to the hospital, dazzled as I cross the Charles River at sunrise. The world is still beautiful.

Holding On:

Intensive Care

Time past and time future
What might have been and what has been
Point to one end, which is always present.

T. S. Eliot, "Burnt Norton"

BEFORE WE VISITED SARAH in New York, Tom and I had been in Cambridge for our thirtieth-anniversary college reunion and to spend time with Martin, who was starting his second year at Harvard. We stayed with Clint, who lives a few blocks from Harvard Square. We went to Martin's large lecture classes, met his friends, and watched him play Ultimate Frisbee.

MARTIN TOOK A year off before starting college. After working hard in high school, he wanted a break from academic pressure. Tom wasn't sure the break was a good idea, given all the temptations available to an eighteen-year-old. This was one rare time when he was more anxious than I. Martin got a job at an outdoor sporting equipment store just off Santa Fe's plaza; took a Spanish class; and enrolled in the local community college's course to become an emergency medical technician (EMT) so he could work as a ski patroller at the local ski area. He went rock climbing and played Ultimate Frisbee. With his savings, he traveled on his own through Mexico from April until August.

A year later, when Martin started college, Tom and I went to the fall parents' weekend. At one gathering, a professor urged us parents not to force our own hopes onto our children. She warned against pushing them to become scientists, or computer experts, or lawyers, or doctors—paths many parents hoped for. Tom and I liked her message.

A questionnaire asked entering students what subjects they planned to major in. Martin, I later learned, was among the one percent who checked *undecided*. At the end of his first year, when he had to choose a field of concentration, he went for Folklore and Mythology. The department is so small it offers, as options for meeting its requirements, several courses from other departments—including Religion, Music, and Fine Arts. Picking Folklore and Mythology as his major left Martin open to a wealth of experience, even if it didn't set him on a course toward a well-paid profession.

ON OUR LAST night in Cambridge after the reunion, Tom and I took Martin out to supper. He told us he wanted to study in Havana next fall. Harvard University was in the process of getting a United States Treasury Department license that would allow faculty and students to travel to Cuba.

At the end of his year off after high school, he had spent a month in Havana, drumming, learning Cuban rhythms from a student from the *Instituto de Artes y Musica*. The Harvard Folklore and Mythology department considered ethnomusicology a legitimate focus for its students, and Martin imagined satisfying his thirst for Cuban music while getting college credit. He was excited by the possibility of living in Havana as a student.

After supper, we had a family hug on the sidewalk, and I stroked Martin's lean face with my hand. I watched him cross the busy street back toward his Lowell House room.

WE WENT TO visit our daughter in New York. Our last night, we saw a play. During the last act, Sarah gripped my hand. Her eyes were wet. Much later, she will tell me that she was suddenly, inexplicably, overwhelmed with grief. I still wonder—was she so tuned in to her brother that, not knowing why, she wept at the moment he was hit?

Sarah's feelings are always close to the surface. She suffers her friends' sorrows and celebrates their successes and joys. When she was born, she opened her eyes wide. In the delivery room's bright lights, she quivered at the sounds and smells of life outside the womb.

As a child, Sarah talked early, and she kept talking. She told me when her brother wanted to nurse, when he needed his diaper changed, and when he wanted me to read to him. Martin talked later, perhaps because Sarah took care of telling me what he needed.

There were years when Martin annoyed his sister. One Saturday morning, Tom asked, "Who wants to come with me on my errands?"

Sarah said, "I'll come if Martin stays home with Mom. If he goes with Dad, I'll stay with Mom."

Martin said, "I'll do whatever Sarah does."

In high school, Martin was the quiet freshman with the backpack full of books, Sarah the senior with friends in every circle. One afternoon in the parking lot, a tough kid, whose jeans sagged below his boxers, glared at skinny Martin. "You're lucky you're Sarah's brother or I would beat you up," he said.

It was no surprise that she chose New York City for college. We worried that she threw herself into the life there too completely, spending too much time in bars and too little on her courses. After Sarah graduated, she spent the summer in Santa Fe, installing exhibits at the Museum of New Mexico. We thought the forty-hour week was good for her. She didn't.

In the fall, she went back to Manhattan and worked at odd jobs. Then the BBC's New York business bureau, where she had worked as an intern in college, offered her a full-time job that October.

Déjà Vu

The Child is the father of the Man . . . .

William Wordsworth, *"My Heart Leaps Up"*

AN IV IS TAPED to Martin's arm, and monitors all over his body record his respiration, his heartbeat, his oxygen level, and the pressure in his brain. Anxious and agitated, he pulls out the IV. The nurse ties his hands to the bed rails.

Martin has been intubated since the medics rescued him on Memorial Drive four days ago. An endotracheal tube still goes down his windpipe. A machine breathes for him. We are not there when he bites through the tube's mouthpiece. When we next see him, they have intubated him once again. Now they have taped the mouthpiece to his face so he can't bite through it.

Tom and I play jazz on a portable CD player Martin's roommate has brought to the hospital. We want to reconnect Martin to himself.

Martin began playing the saxophone in fourth grade. He first went to an overnight music camp when he was nine, and he went there every summer after that, trying the trombone, electric bass, piano, and drums. In tenth grade, he found a summer program at Boston's Berklee School of Music, probably in a magazine. I felt inadequate when he showed me the brochures and the application form he'd sent away for. *He doesn't need me to figure this out for him,* I thought. *He's finding his own way.*

THAT WAS NOT the first time Martin presented us with a decision, having left us out of whatever process he went through to reach it. Nor was it the last time he was cryptic. Near the end of high school, on May first, the day he had to mail his letter to the college he had chosen, he went to the post office minutes before it would close. As he walked out of our house, Martin told us he still had not made up his mind on which college he would choose. When he came home, he said he'd picked Harvard—because, he said, when he looked over the paperwork, he noticed that Stanford wanted a check, and he didn't have his checkbook. He never changed his story.

IN HIGH SCHOOL, Martin played his saxophone in a band. The musicians performed in bars they were all too young to go into as customers. I often found him in his room, eyes closed, listening to jazz, Cuban salsa music, or the blues.

With the ET tube down his windpipe, Martin can't speak, but now, when he is not sedated, he follows us with wide open eyes. Since he blinked to show he could hear us, we have helped him communicate by blinking. We ask him to blink once if he wants Miles Davis's *Kind of Blue*, twice if not. When he wants to sleep, he blinks twice and we turn off the music.

The nurses say Martin must have reality as his anchor: date, time, place, facts. Since the first day we have been telling him, "You were hit by a car. An ambulance brought you to Massachusetts General Hospital. You are doing very well. We have been with you all the time, and you are very strong. You have great doctors and nurses. We love you." Reality—and hope.

I OFTEN THINK about how children are far more tuned in than their parents know. When one hears her mother say, "She doesn't like anything but macaroni and pizza," it's a green light for her not to eat anything but macaroni and pizza. If she says, "He hasn't had that before, but he'll probably like it," he'll try something new. I warn young friends with small children, "Be careful what you say; they don't miss a thing."

I think the same way about people who are seriously ill. When someone is unconscious, whether sedated or in a coma, you should not voice your worry. Talk about the living world, where wind blows the trees and the air smells green. Talk about your hopes for the future. What you project is what the patient will perceive.

NOTHING COULD HAVE prepared me for this precipice between hope and fear.

But I have been with a brain trauma patient in an ICU before.

Sarah was seven weeks old when my father skidded on a patch of ice and fell off his bicycle onto his head. The doctor sent him home, never telling my mother to watch out for confusion, distress, or personality changes. By the time she became alarmed, a week later, great damage had been done.

With Sarah in my arms, I flew through the night from Albuquerque to somewhere in the Midwest. I felt I was heading into a long dark tunnel, with no idea of when, if ever, I would come out into the light. We flew on to Newark. To keep Sarah swallowing so her ears wouldn't hurt with the air pressure changes, I nursed her for two thousand miles.

On the winter morning when we landed, the sun was shining.

While Daddy was in the hospital, magic hands cared for my mother and me. We came home from the ICU to dishes that had been washed and put away, beds that were made, and clean diapers hanging on the clothesline. My baby slept, calmed by the lullabies my mother's friends sang to her.

Mother had always cared for others who needed help—bringing meals, caring for children, driving friends whose ankles or wrists were sprained or broken. She invited newcomers for tea or drinks, introducing them to her friends with similar interests. When people came to town to meet with my father, he brought them home. Over a meal my mother cooked, he learned more about them than he could have at a restaurant or in his office.

After two surgeries, four good years, one year of losing his mind, and four terrible years of dementia, Daddy died. I handled those last years badly. I lost myself in daydreams, wanted to run away, and tried any escape—marijuana, romantic fantasies, writing poetry. I could do nothing for my father. Some mornings I woke sobbing. When Tom tried to wake me from my nightmare, I told him, *I'm not dreaming, I'm awake.* He could not rescue me, and I thought I was alone. Unable to reach me, he must have felt abandoned too.

I still miss my father. Sometimes I see him in his grandson—the bird-like tilt of the head, a moment's silliness, the long time Martin takes to consider before he speaks. I wear Daddy's navy windbreaker so often the cuffs have frayed. I wrap his brown wool scarf around me when I'm cold.

My father came to this country from Germany in 1935. Although his Jewish parents had become Lutherans when they married, it was clear that he had no future there. Nine years later, during World War II, he went back to Germany as an American army intelligence officer. After teaching German in American colleges, he knew to make a few mistakes speaking German so the prisoners he interrogated would not realize that he had been born and grown up in Germany. With them, he played the role of a well-educated native-born American. Understanding the quirks of Germans of particular social classes or from certain towns or areas of Germany, he often guessed their little secrets. When he did, they thought he could read their minds and they reckoned they might as well tell him bigger secrets. They were relieved to find a sympathetic American officer who understood them.

I never heard Daddy express hatred toward the Germans. After the war, Rotary International sent him around the United States. He gave talks about Western Europe to high school students by day and to their parents and other townspeople by night. He wanted Americans to understand the fear and desperation Germany had experienced after the First World War, when he was a child and a young man. He wanted them to know that Germans were not monsters, but fellow human beings who deserved compassion.

For years I wondered whether Daddy was hiding his true

feelings. Now I think that he sought to understand the German people so life would be bearable, and that he knew that hatred only makes the hater small.

After my father's brain injury, melancholy stalked him. He told me, "I feel like a black dog is sitting on my chest." Daddy had always been afraid of dogs, although he knew his fears were unreasonable. He said he must have had a scary experience with a dog as a young child, an experience he couldn't remember.

The last time he came to Santa Fe, two or three years after his accident, I sat with him when he lay down to nap. He said, "I just want to lie in a plain pine box and rest."

IN THE YEARS since my father's brain injury, much has changed. At Mass General, Martin's room itself is a work of genius. Its designers talked to the ICU nurses who would work there. A tower in the center of the room runs from the floor to the ceiling. The bed, too, is in the middle of the room, its head beside the power tower. The nurses move freely all around the patient, unhampered by wires or tubes. The tubes that breathe for Martin, the lines that drip medicine into him, and the gauges that measure his pressures and chemistries, all connect to the tower. Like the nurses, we can move in a circle around him, easily keeping out of their way.

On his third day in the hospital, doctors and nurses tell us, "Martin *will* get pneumonia." Because he is sedated, a machine pumps air into his lungs. His exhalations are his own, but he does not push the air out of his lungs with any force.

He does get pneumonia. The hospital lab identifies the

particular pneumococcus strain in his lungs, and they tailor an anti-biotic in order to defeat it.

WE RECENTLY CHANGED health insurance companies. Our agent said the new company would provide excellent coverage, if we ever needed it. To save money, we chose a high deductible of $2500 per person per year.

Our agent tells me that our car insurance pays up to $10,000 for medical bills of "a covered driver" who is injured "as a pedestrian." Martin may use $2500 from the car insurance to pay the health insurance's deductible for each of the next four years.

On top of this unexpected break, the no fault policy of the driver of the car that hit him even provides some extra coverage. We don't need to worry about paying for all the care Martin will need.

ON SUNDAY AFTERNOON, our fifth day at Mass General, Tom and I sit in the waiting room at the shift change. A skinny black man wearing gray coveralls peers in and asks, "Is there a clock in here?"

"No," Tom answers. "Don't you have a watch?"

"I'm setting the hospital's clocks back for fall," he says in a Caribbean lilt, "and, no, I don't have a watch."

He looks straight at us and says, "My body tells me the three things I need to know—when to get up, when to go to sleep, and when to go to the bathroom. That's all I need to know."

He walks away, looking for clocks to change.

Martin's body is finding its own way to heal, despite the

doctors contradicting one another about whether he is or ever has been in a coma, about how long his condition will be critical, about why his intracranial pressure is so high yet he is so responsive. We have begun to trust ourselves, and to settle into waiting, letting Martin set the pace.

Tom and I ask each other whether anyone else has seen the man who sets the clocks, the man who wears no watch and changes time. No one but us has heard his magic words. Perhaps there will be other miracles.

MARTIN HAS ALWAYS moved at his own pace. When he graduated from high school, Sarah made a video of interviews with his friends. Britten, whom he's known since pre-school, laughed as she told about calling him to say she'd pick him up for a movie. He'd tell her, "I'm ready, I just need to put on my shoes," and, when she got there, twenty minutes later, Martin was still putting on his shoes. He had to tie his laces before they could go.

Another friend told the camera how "chilled out" Martin was. She said that, when he drank, he just got quieter and quieter, sitting at the edge of the party, watching everyone else, and nodding to himself.

Martin was even born at his own pace, two weeks late. His fingernails were extra-long, and, because he'd stayed inside so long that he'd lost weight, he looked like a size six baby in a size ten suit of skin, wrinkled and waterlogged. When the doctor looked him over, he finally accepted what I'd been telling him—my baby was way past due.

Martin shut his eyes tight and feigned sleep, or perhaps he truly slept, as soon as he was born. Soon, with his parents and sister walking upright, talking, and using the toilet, he was trying to catch up.

As soon as he could crawl, he grabbed onto my jeans or my long skirt and pulled himself to stand. While I washed dishes, he stood behind me, swaying, until, tired from holding on, he let go and dropped to the floor.

When he began walking, Martin went outside barefoot, wearing a bonnet and a shirt to keep off the sun. The summer he was two, I found him standing by the water hydrant far from the house. He had climbed the big rock step beside the flower bed to reach the handle, turned the water off, carried the sprinkler with the hose it was attached to from the lawn into the house, and set the sprinkler on the floor beside Tom's desk. When I found him, he was back on the step by the hydrant, reaching to turn the water on.

Was I not watching him enough?

Another day, I followed him when he walked from a friend's dining nook into her kitchen. He pushed her step stool over to the counter, climbed up, stood on the counter, and reached for a glass on the cabinet shelf. My friend watched him and then said, "When I talk with you on the phone, and you say that Martin is getting into something, I always think you're slow at keeping track of him. But you're not slow. Martin's just fast."

Fast sometimes, and sometimes slow. He sets his own pace.

After Silence

There is so much kindness.

Martin, after his endotracheal tube is removed.

O N THE SIXTH DAY, Monday, the neurosurgeon finally says that Martin no longer needs sedation. Dr. Hammer thinks he is strong enough to breathe on his own and that it is safe to remove the endotracheal tube.

As always, we leave the room while the doctors do a medical procedure. When the nurse calls us back in, Martin tries to speak. We can't understand his whisper.

Clint has told us of permanent harm done to vocal chords of patients who had difficult intubations. The paramedics had to intubate Martin two times before they got him to Mass General. Later, in the hospital, Martin pulled out the tube and was intubated a third time. We are afraid his vocal chords may be damaged.

Tom puts his ear by Martin's mouth. He repeats every sound he hears him make. Martin struggles to form sounds we can understand. Three feet away, I cannot hear him. Suddenly Tom's face lights up. He repeats what he has heard: "What happened?" After so many days of silence, we are overwhelmed to hear him speak.

Tom repeats what we have been saying from the beginning: "You were hit by a car. They brought you by ambulance to Massachusetts General Hospital. You are doing well. We have been with you all the time, and you are strong. You have great doctors and nurses."

"How long?" Martin rasps.

Tom answers, "It's been six days."

Martin says, "Wow." His response is so apt, we are euphoric.

Martin touches his face and asks, "Who shaved me?" We are amazed at how clearly he now speaks, mere minutes after struggling to form words we could understand. And he is making connections: six days, I am clean shaven, therefore someone must have shaved me.

"The nurses," we answer in unison.

"At Mass General?" he asks.

"Yes," we say.

Martin says his head aches, and we tell him we will ask the nurse to bring him some Tylenol. He says, "There is so much kindness."

While we are waiting for the nurse, Martin says, "Maybe we should go and take the Tylenol at home." We tell him we can't go home yet, and he asks us, "Tell me again what happened." We do.

Later, he looks at the power tower beside his bed and asks what it is. We explain that its gauges measure his blood pressure, his heartbeat, his respiration, his oxygen level, and the pressure inside his brain. He says, "I'm glad I'm an EMT."

"Because you understand what's happening?" I ask.

"Yes," he says.

Martin is tired. He sleeps.

NEAR THE END of Martin's course to become an EMT in the fall after he finished high school, he rode with a local ambulance service. There was a lot of time sitting around waiting for calls, with only the occasional medical transport, driving someone from a nursing home to the hospital for dialysis and taking the patient back to the home.

One cold morning, Martin asked us which jacket he should take for his shift at Rocky Mountain Emergency Medical Services. Tom said, "Wear your winter parka, and take your lighter jacket for later in the day, when it gets warmer."

In the office at Rocky Mountain EMS, a call came in. The two paramedics ran for the ambulance. Martin barely had time to grab his jackets and climb in back. On the drive, they told him that their chief paramedic was driving to town with his wife when a pickup crossed the solid yellow lines and hit their car head on. Charles had called his own accident in to the dispatcher.

At the accident scene, Martin gave one of his jackets to a volunteer medic who had none. The paramedics tended to Charles's wife and to the Mexican man whose pickup had caused the crash. Charles, Rocky Mountain's injured paramedic, walked around, directing the other medics. Martin helped by translating for the Mexican until the volunteers loaded him into their ambulance. When both Rocky Mountain's paramedics wanted to ride in back to take care of Charles and his wife, Martin drove the ambulance to the hospital.

That evening, Martin told us the story. Tom was amazed at

how he had been able to uncouple his feelings from the work that had to be done. Martin explained that he had been expressly trained to function under stress, learning routines by heart so he would overlook nothing. Much more than the tag-along he expected to be, he had provided a needed jacket, translated for an injured patient, and driven the ambulance.

The doctors at the hospital pronounced Charles well enough to go home, and kept his wife overnight for observation.

Two years later, while Martin is in Mass General, I call a woman whom our Cambridge friend Josefina knows, a woman whose son-in-law suffered a head injury in Santa Fe. As I listen to her story, I realize that her son-in-law is the paramedic Martin drove to the hospital. Charles now suffers from headaches and depression. The doctors who said he was fine were wrong. His head had hit the windshield, and he had *delayed onset traumatic brain injury*.

A PAMPHLET FROM the National Institute of Neurological Disorders and Stroke, gives an overview of TBI:

> TBI . . . occurs when a sudden trauma causes damage to the brain. The damage can be focal—confined to one area of the brain—or diffuse—involving more than one area of the brain. TBI can result from a *closed head injury* ... or a *penetrating head injury*. A closed injury occurs when the head suddenly and violently hits an object but the object does not break through the skull. A penetrating injury occurs when an object pierces the skull and enters brain tissue. . . . Sometimes when the brain is injured swelling occurs and fluids accumulate within the brain space. It is

normal for bodily injuries to cause swelling and disruptions in fluid balance. But when an injury occurs inside the skull-encased brain, there is no place for swollen tissues to expand and no adjoining tissues to absorb excess fluid. This increased pressure is called *intracranial pressure (ICP)*.

After my father hit his head, spinal fluid accumulated between his skull and his brain, restricting blood flow and oxygen to the brain. It took six days for my mother to realize something was seriously wrong. After his second surgery, Daddy could not speak for eleven days. Less than three months later, he prepared his own tax return. Then, four years later, dementia began.

How does TBI happen? Countless ways. What does TBI lead to? Countless outcomes. With TBI, all you can count on is unpredictability.

AFTER MARTIN RESTS, he wants to talk more. He asks, "Have you met Dave?" We tell him that we ate supper with him and his roommate Dave a week before the accident, and that Dave has been coming to Mass General to visit us.

After his brain injury, my father did not remember that I had had a child. He did not remember that he was a grandfather, that Sarah existed. She was born seven weeks before his accident, and his memory of a stretch of time before and after his accident was completely gone.

I am not surprised that Martin's memory has voids.

We were in Cambridge just a week before his accident. We watched him and his roommate play Ultimate Frisbee in the rain. When Dave leaped for a catch, he flew horizontally. As I watched him diving and crashing in the mud, I said to Tom how glad I was that Dave was not our son—the worry would be too great.

Now, in the hospital, Martin asks, "What do you think of Dave?"

I say, "He's quiet and doesn't let on much, but there's amazing brightness and there's the energy I saw at Ultimate."

Martin says, "It's often like that."

I ask, "That amazing people don't show a lot on the surface?"

He says, "Yes. Have you met Rachel?"

During our week in Cambridge, we went to supper with Rachel, whom Martin met a year ago. Behind her social composure, Rachel watches everyone intensely. Martin, always private, had said just enough to make us wonder if he was in love with her. After Sarah met her last spring, she said, "If Rachel hurts my brother, I'll kill her."

We tell Martin that we know Rachel, and that she has visited us in the hospital.

After a few minutes, Martin suggests we let the nurse know that we have moved.

I tell him, "We haven't moved. We're where we've always been. The nurse is helping someone else and will come here when she's done." Now that Martin is no longer sedated or intubated, his nurse has been assigned another patient to care for as well.

Martin says, "We should let her know where we are."

I repeat that we haven't moved, but that the nurse has left the room.

He says, "I doubt you." He adds, "Time is confusing."

"Yes it is," I say. "Do you remember you were taking a course on Einstein?"

He says, "I still am."

Confused and forgetful, he is nevertheless tuned to the nuances of verb tenses, curious about his surroundings, concerned that we show consideration for his nurse, and self-observant. He is aware that his time sense is confused, he imagines possible scenarios, and he empathizes with his nurse. At some level, we sense that many of his higher faculties are intact, but we do not yet know enough to understand the significance of what we are witnessing. Less than a week after his accident, Martin does not seem to face many of the direst scenarios of traumatic brain injury.

> Disabilities resulting from TBI . . . include problems with cognition (thinking, memory, and reasoning), sensory processing (sight, hearing, touch, taste, and smell), communication (expression and understanding), and behavior or mental health (depression, anxiety, personality changes, aggression, acting out, and social inappropriateness). [From "Hope Through Research," the National Institute of Neurological Disorders and Stroke].

MUCH LATER, READING my notes from conversations we had in the ICU, I see that I was expanding on Martin's responses, reminding him of more that he knew or that he might be thinking. Perhaps my prodding helped him reconnect with his own complex mind.

My conversations with my children, when they were two and three and four years old, did the same thing—starting from what they said, stretching their idea with my response, tossing the conversation back and forth, creating often unexpected variations on their themes.

This is how you grow a child. This is how you start to heal a brain.

I AM EAGER to discover more of what Martin still knows. I ask Maria, the Portuguese woman who mops the floor in his room, if she speaks Spanish. She does. Martin responds to her simple greeting in fluent Spanish. Tom arrives while I am listening to their conversation.

"This is my papa," Martin tells Maria, in English.

"How nice," Maria says. "Your mother and father are both here."

"Mother and father," he replies, "the best of both worlds."

It is Martin's first figure of speech, a milestone we had not been looking for.

Learning to Wait:
In the Land of Oz

. . . that year I learned the odds are that nothing can keep you safe. So many concurrent painful events altered our sense of each one, just as a color appears to change when another color is placed beside it.

Francine Prose, *"Talking Dog," The Peaceable Kingdom*

T OM AND I WORK as real estate brokers. We've had our own company for over twenty years, and it's just the two of us. Almost all of our clients come from referrals. We have a little office in town, but we often work from home. With telephones and modern technology, we can take care of much of our small business from afar.

We have also bought several houses, houses that scared off other buyers. Sarah was two and a half when she named "Hail House" for the mounds of hail she watched Tom shovel out the door of a just bought house with a roof full of just discovered holes. We've done most of the fix up ourselves, and then sold the houses or kept them as rentals.

Because neither of us has a regular job, we can stay in Boston with Martin. Sarah's friends in Santa Fe, women in their early twenties, will feed our cats, water our plants, and bring in our mail.

THE DOCTORS HAVE at last stopped sedating Martin and have taken out his ET tube. Still, at the end of the first week, the neurosurgeon is waiting for Martin's intracranial pressure (ICP) to come down so he can take the pressure relief tube out of his brain.

"Martin is so bright," Dr. Hammer says, meaning his responsiveness, not his intelligence, "that the ICP reading is likely artifactual."

"What does that mean?" Tom and I ask.

"Perhaps," the neurosurgeon says, "the reading is not to be credited." He continues, rapid fire, anxious to be rid of us, "One cannot be so bright, so appropriately responsive as Martin is, with the pressure that the ICP reading shows."

We still do not understand precisely what *artifactual* means, but we know Martin is doing better than the green numbers say. A day later, Dr. Hammer takes out the pressure relief tube.

For Tom, the neurosurgeon's indifference to our puzzlement is a revelation. He says, "You're on your knees in front of the medical system and then—*PAY NO ATTENTION TO THAT MAN BEHIND THE CURTAIN!* You discover you're in Oz and there is no great or powerful Oz who knows what is going on."

All the hours while Martin lay unconscious, sedated or sleeping, we stared at the green numbers that reported his blood pressure, his respiration, his oxygen level, and his ICP. We took them as gospel. Then suddenly the curtain blew to the side and we glimpsed, in Tom's words, "what the medical community knows and thinks you common people don't have to know, that you're not privileged enough to understand, that you wouldn't understand." We realized what they knew all along but did not tell us—that no one had any certainty about what was happening or going to happen with Martin.

Much later we learn more about artifactual readings. The neurosurgeon thought the ICP gauge could have been a few millimeters off where it should have been, or that it was touching something that distorted the reading of the pressure in Martin's brain. To Dr. Hammer, these possibilities are unremarkable. We wish he had explained them to us.

I AM AMAZED how passive we were. At times, I have been called a warrior, often as criticism, sometimes as praise.

I have done battle for my children. One Friday afternoon, Martin, in line for the school bus home, threw a water balloon. We weren't home when the principal called to tell us he was keeping our son until we came to get him. The man told our ten-year-old that if he couldn't reach us, he would have to stay alone at school until Monday.

When we got the principal's message we rushed to the school. Martin was in tears. Tom had listened to my tales of this principal's bullying for years, and now he had had enough. He wrote on a yellow pad for hours. His notes became the catalyst for a record of the principal's abuse of power. Mothers and fathers who had lived through their children's mistreatment told me their stories. I edited their tales into a document we presented to the school superintendent. The school board later held a hearing, with parents describing bullying of teachers, parents, and children. The school board dodged the issue, and created a paper-heavy bureaucratic process that was supposed to help the principal mend his ways. Yet they left him in charge. Almost three years later, teachers complained that the principal was harassing them. He was sacked. I think our earlier outspokenness gave the teachers the courage to speak up, courage they had not had before.

So, why were Tom and I so deferential to the doctors? Did our unspoken fears keep us from confronting them, from demanding that they tell us what they thought?

We should have spoken up.

AFTER MY FATHER'S brain surgery in 1976, no flowers were allowed in the ICU and our house overflowed with bouquets. I put my long hair up and pinned flowers to my head. I walked into my father's ICU room haloed in lilies and roses, freesias and irises, all the blossoms our friends had sent. I was my father's bouquet.

A card from Josie, Martin's high school friend, with a picture of a sunflower:

Martin—

Since real flowers are not allowed in the room I thought a picture might be the next best thing. It is only a small token of how much I care for you. I would fill your room with all the flowers in the world if I could. You are in my daily thought, Martin. I love you very, very much. And although I am across the country, know that I am here for you in every way possible. All you have to do is close your eyes and remember the two of us sitting on top of Sun

Mountain watching the sun set and basking in the company of each other; and there I will be, right beside you, getting ready to climb the next mountain. I LOVE YOU.

WHEN HIS NURSE is assigned a second patient, Tom and I worry that she will not be able to keep Martin safe, because she has to leave his room to tend to the other patient. We cannot imagine how one nurse can care for two patients. By the time Martin leaves Intensive Care, his assigned nurse is caring for three.

At times during his week in Intensive Care, the nurses are strident about being in charge. We are careful, asking many questions, but keeping silent when the nurse is working. The nurses are like good pilots, flying by instinct and instruments, occasionally coasting, but always alert and ready for turbulence. They teach us which medications do what, what the gauges' green numbers signify, and what goes on when Martin is taken away for tests. They explain to us what we are waiting for—reduction of the sedative, removal of the ventilator, decrease in the intracranial pressure, and improvements in heart rate and blood pressure. When we mention conversations we have had with one doctor or another, they provide some insights. A nurse declaring "Oh he's always like that" illuminates a great deal for us. Tom says it is like hearing servants talk about their employers – the nurses know the doctors better than the doctors know themselves.

What is it about some doctors? Is it the years they spent in training, the inhuman hours they worked as interns, their medical school debts? Their knowledge is vast, they are overworked, and it's hard to explain much to a layman—but sometimes they seem not to care that the patient, or the patient's family, wants to know what is happening and the possible outcomes. They sometimes seem unaware that there are those, with little medical knowledge and no Latin, who are even more concerned than the doctors themselves are, concerned about what happens to the body that they, the doctors, just happen to be in charge of.

TOM AND I develop routines. We leave the ICU at shift changes, at doctors' rounds, and when Martin is washed or taken from the ICU for x-rays and CAT scans. His nurse travels everywhere with him. Going for an x-ray means converting all the monitoring equipment, the oxygen and the ventilator, the pressure relief valve and all the other high tech tools, to mobile systems. We are not allowed to be in the room then.

For several days, I eat Indian food Martin's friend has brought from his Boston family, as well as whatever Tom carries up from the cafeteria. The Mass General kitchen has been honored for its healthy, delicious, and extensive choice of meals. Thousands eat there each day, many with no connection to the hospital. They come for lunch because it is close to their work, and the food is excellent.

Tom pilots me through the cafeteria my first time. I almost believe that, as he joked earlier, Central Casting has sent over hundreds of extras just to mill about the hospital. A day later, I am brave enough to approach the specialty grill and the enormous salad bar on my own.

In the waiting room, we talk with Joanne. She arrived at the ICU the day we did. A truck had hit her husband as he was pulling out of their driveway. Joanne didn't notice us in her first days at Mass

General and we were barely aware of her. But eventually we see each other. We hear her talking with her mother and her young daughter on the waiting room telephone.

On Saturday, Joanne leaves a note on the bulletin board saying she has gone home to Nantucket and will return Sunday night. We buy Post-it notes and take messages from her friends who call. We leave notes saying where we are and when we will be back:

> *4 pm Sunday, Tom and Elise are in ICU with Martin.*
> *Please leave a message.*

and

> *2:45 Monday, Tom and Elise in cafeteria in basement. Back*
> *here by 3:30. Please take messages.*

It seems incredible that Mass General has no system for messages in the waiting room. We don't know what calls or visitors we've missed already. Now everyone uses the Post-it notes we brought.

We begin to notice others who are also waiting. We learn their stories. It is as if we all arrived deaf and blind, in a trance, completely alone. Then the clouds began to lift, we saw one another, and eventually we spoke.

A woman has come from St. Louis. She did extensive research before choosing Mass General for her son's brain surgery. Her husband is still in St. Louis. Tom and I talk about how hard it must be for her to be here alone. We are grateful for each other.

One woman in the ICU has a tumor surrounding her auditory nerve. Her physician husband tells us that, although they have lived in England for years, they kept their American health insurance. They chose Mass General for her surgery.

People with time to research hospitals picked Mass General for their neurosurgeries. We are thankful that the paramedics brought Martin here.

AFTER MARTIN'S ET tube is taken out, a speech therapist arrives. She explains that speech therapists concentrate on everything that happens above the shoulders—swallowing and mental functioning as well as speech. She has been called to assess whether Martin can be given food or drink by mouth. She concludes that he might aspirate his food, and, because aspiration could lead to a new respiratory infection, declares that he cannot be fed orally.

Martin was thin before the accident, and he hasn't eaten anything for six days. One option, intravenous feeding, has a high risk of infection. To feed him, a nurse inserts a nasogastric tube through his nose down the back of his throat into his stomach. Even with his hands tied to the bed rails, he manages to pull the tube out by bending his head forward and hooking the tube with his thumb. Each option—oral feeding, intravenous feeding, nasogastric tube—has its own unique dangers. Yet Martin is so weak that doing nothing is dangerous. Tom and I talk in circles, as if by talking we might find a solution to the feeding impasse, something that no one else has thought of. We feel trapped, with no way out.

Martin's nurse on Monday, the sixth night, is an older woman. Tom has seen her leafing through retirement magazines. After she promises to telephone if Martin needs us, I leave with Tom to go sleep at Clint's. It is the first night neither of us has stayed at the hospital. At four a.m., I wake and call the ICU.

"Martin is sleeping," his nurse says. "He just ate some pudding. He seemed ready to eat, so I gave it a try. He did fine."

Her common sense has trumped the speech therapist's caution. Close to retirement, she knows when to take no notice of the higher authorities. I wake Tom to tell him. Joyful, we sleep until six.

TO KEEP BLOOD clots from forming in his legs while Martin is in bed, one doctor orders air pressure boots. The pump under the bed inflates the boots around his calves, squeezing the blood back toward his heart. His legs turn dark red with bruises. In the quiet ICU, the pump sounds like a dragon asleep in a cave, breathing long slow hisses.

I REMEMBER A lesson Martin's EMT instructor in Santa Fe taught. She told the class about a patient whose EKG readings were ragged and "funky," but he was sitting up talking with her, feeling fine. "Treat the patient," she said, "not the machine."

If I'd remembered that story sooner, maybe Dr. Hammer's baffling *artifactual* would have made more sense. He was treating the machine, perplexed that his patient was doing so well.

Of course, a patient's recovery from brain trauma is not simple, and machines are doctors' invaluable partners. There is no map a doctor can follow, no sure way to reconcile contrary signs. Every case is different.

A card from a college friend of Martin's:

> . . . *I've learned many things through physical trials. Probably*

*the most important was that God uses them to bring us closer
to Him. They condition our mind into thinking beyond our
physical body to what else is to come.*

My thoughts are so bound to Martin's physical body that this
loving card annoys me. Later, its wisdom astounds me.

IN THE WAITING room, a Greek woman and her teenage
niece and nephew talk in whispers with a young Greek Orthodox priest.
They cry a lot. The woman's brother, the teenagers' father, has brain
cancer. One day the woman is standing there alone. Her brother has
died. She feels terrible, she says, because she told him everything would
be all right. I believe she told him the truth: now he is finally out of
pain; his children were with him when he died; and she will care for
them and keep his memory alive.

"When you reassured your brother, you did not know what all
right was going to mean," I tell her, "and now you do." We hold each
other for several minutes. I think of the night I helped myself to sleep by
murmuring, "Martin will be well."

I still don't know if Martin will get better.

I know we are missing a great deal of what goes on in the ICU.
Families of the dying spend only the briefest moments in the waiting
room. I know there are back passages and elevators because, when they
take Martin away for tests, he does not come through the main door.
Patients who die must be taken out a back way, and their families leave
so quickly and silently that, except for the Greek woman, we do not
encounter them.

Two large groups of people spend time in the waiting room.

The first group looks angry all the time. They sit so close to the telephone that I feel awkward using it. Despite our Post-it notes, they don't take messages, and they snipe at one another. Dying might seem preferable to going home with them. They make me sympathize with the ICU's tight rules about who can be in the patient's room and when. Visitors can get in the way of nurses. Some visitors will distress the patients. The rules protect the nurses and the patients.

I am grateful that the nurses bend the rules for Tom and me. Except for when they convert the monitoring equipment to mobile systems and for the frenzied times of shift changes and doctors' rounds, we stay with Martin.

A second large group arrives on Martin's last day in the ICU. As many as sixteen at a time, they speak Portuguese, and many talk at once. They are like a village, ready to go down to the sea, jump in a boat together, and cast their nets for fish. We believe that whoever they are there for will get well, if only to rejoin them.

We hope that Martin will come back to us.

AT THE SHIFT change one afternoon, we find Martin's roommate, Dave, sitting in the waiting room with Melanie. Melanie went to Santa Fe's Catholic high school before coming to Harvard, but we have not met her before. Tom leaves on an errand, and I invite Joanne, the Nantucket woman whose husband is in the ICU, to come with us to the cafeteria. Melanie and I entertain Dave and Joanne with stories of Santa Fe. We tell them that only fifty-four percent of the students who enter Santa Fe High School graduate four years later. Martin has already overcome considerable odds to arrive at Harvard from Santa Fe High.

A letter addressed to "Martin —, Patient, Massachusetts General Hospital":

Dear Martin,

. . . I live in the Master's residence at Winthrop House. I am on the fourth floor and am rarely home as I have to travel quite often for my job. I happened to be home last Tuesday night and was doing my bills. At around 11, I heard the terrible noise and looked out to see your accident. From that moment on, I just prayed and prayed for your life and for your well-being and for your family and for the people in the car. I called an ambulance and they were there very quickly. I kept praying while they were treating you and have prayed for you all during the week. I was so pleased to see in the Crimson [the student newspaper] that you had been upgraded to fair condition.

I just wanted you to know that there are many people who prayed for you that night and will continue to pray for you and your family during your recovery.

Best wishes for a speedy recuperation.

Early Lessons—The Thinnest Thread: Santa Fe, New Mexico

> *I learned from my mother how to love*
> *the living, to have plenty of vases on hand*
> *in case you have to rush to the hospital*
> *with peonies cut from the lawn . . . .*
> *I learned that whatever we say means nothing,*
> *what anyone will remember is that we came.*

> *Julia Kasdorf, "What I learned from My Mother"*

A LONG TIME AGO, my father suffered his terrible head injury. Then, only ten weeks before Martin's accident, in late summer, I fractured my skull. Martin and Tom and I were helping my mother move into her new apartment, just three miles from our home.

LATE TO MEET friends who want to buy a house, I run back up to Mother's new retirement apartment for my cell phone. Tom and Martin are tallying the boxes the movers carry in. I am angry that they act as if only I can supervise her move. I blame them for keeping me from leaving sooner. In my rush, I have left my phone on the window sill.

Cell phone in hand, I run to make up time. Halfway down the courtyard stairs, I start to fly. I try to grab the railing, and spin, fly backwards, tumbling. My head hits concrete. Tom and Martin watch from upstairs. Then they are beside me. I hear Martin tell someone to call 911 for an ambulance. He holds my head.

A nurse from the retirement complex's medical center arrives. Martin tells her to bring oxygen. She says, "Your mother doesn't need oxygen."

He says, "Bring the oxygen."

Later, he explains that medical protocols decree that the person at the patient's head is in charge. He knows I should have oxygen. Decades younger than the nurse, he holds my head and stays in charge. He starts oxygen for me, deferring to no one until a paramedic he trusts arrives.

Six medics care for me at the bottom of the stairs. They hoist me onto a stretcher. Looking up at the sky and trying to breathe over the pain, I see only Martin. He rides in the ambulance with me. Tom drives our car to the hospital.

We live a mile beyond the hospital, in the house we bought twenty years ago, just before Martin was born. I know every inch of the journey, but the pain is too great for me to track our progress. Coming down the hill to the last traffic light, the ambulance tilts me head downward, and I realize we are close. I hear the lead paramedic on her radio, telling the hospital we are almost there.

In the emergency room, nurses keep looking into my cubicle.

Tom asks each one to bring a doctor immediately. We hear people singing *Happy Birthday*. The doctor we are hoping for is probably eating cake and ice cream. Forty-five minutes pass before she comes to me.

My eye sockets are turning red and purple. Because Martin is a medic, the nurses let him stay beside me as they wheel me through the corridors. X-rays and scans tell them that, in spite of my raccoon eyes, an indication that my skull is fractured, I most likely will be all right.

I spend the night in the hospital, so nurses can watch over me.

The next day, at home, I stay in bed. I rest for days. My head throbs. The yippings of the little dogs next door feel like knives in my brain.

It is three weeks before I drive, and Mother survives the passage to a retirement apartment without my help. This was not my plan.

MAUREEN WAS A war bride. She met my father on her London doorstep, on the day my parents always called *D-Day Plus One*—June 6, 1945. Hans was an American Intelligence officer; she a young English woman who'd spent the war working in London. They married six months later.

Maureen had lived in France after she finished school. First, she looked after the children of a family outside Paris. Then she became the au pair for an American journalist and his wife, who lived in Paris. She cared for their little boy during the day and had the evenings she had dreamed of, meeting other young people in cafés and dancing past midnight. Later, she found ways to stay in Paris, tutoring French businessmen in English, subsisting, she told me, on good French bread and ketchup she stirred into cups of hot water to make tomato soup.

In the spring of 1939, knowing that war was coming, Maureen returned to England. She made some money as a model; I have photographs of her wearing a tweed suit, smiling a little as she sits on a stone wall, crossing her lovely legs. She stayed in London through the war, and worked as a press censor.

The American journalist, whose son she had cared for in Paris, reported from London for the *Herald Tribune*. Through him, Maureen met other journalists. She spent evenings at the Savoy Hotel, after-hours headquarters for journalists, and often walked home through London's dark streets after the underground trains stopped running. One night she watched as fire burned the famous churches of St. Clement Dane and St. Mary-le-Strand.

Sometimes it seems that Sarah is living a life much like young Maureen's, deep in the culture of trans-Atlantic journalism, burning both ends of the candle.

Only recently did my mother tell me that, for some of those years, she had a lover, a Canadian journalist whose wife and son were back in Canada. Matt and Maureen were known as a couple, and they and the friends in their circle all understood that, after the war, Matt would go back to Canada and his family.

Mother's world was like nothing I have known. Everyone knew that war was coming long before it came, the American continent was more than a week away by ship, trans-Atlantic telephone calls were rare, and pilots you drank with in the evening flew off early the next day and might be dead by noon.

When the war ended in Europe, Matt went home to Canada, and someone introduced Maureen to Hans, the man she would marry—my father.

Her first home in America was Colorado Springs. Hans had started teaching at Colorado College in 1938, three years after he came to the United States. After the war, he traveled the country giving talks about Western Europe, and my pregnant mother waited, hemming baby blankets in their tiny Brooklyn apartment.

When I was ten, Daddy became director of an educational foundation in Princeton, New Jersey.

Mother began work at the New Jersey Neuropsychiatric Institute, driving through the wooded countryside several days a week. Years before, she had edited entries for Columbia University Press's desktop encyclopedia. At the Neuropsychiatric Institute, she translated impenetrable medical studies into prose even the uninitiated could understand.

Daddy drove me to school most mornings. Mother picked me up. We had tea together, with bread and honey for me, before I started my many hours of homework. Some evenings, as the day was fading, she called me to come, right away. We would drive to a rise beside an open field and watch brilliant sunsets, rare in often overcast New Jersey.

AFTER MY FATHER'S death, before we persuaded her to come to Santa Fe, Mother moved back to Colorado Springs, her first American home. It was an easy five-hour drive to visit me, her only child. I helped her find a house near the college, a few blocks from where she and Daddy had lived. She had old friends there, and made new ones.

A couple who taught at the college lived two houses away.

They kept their second car in Mother's big attached garage, and their guests from out of town slept in Mother's guest room. In return, they invited Mother to dinners with their visiting friends and family. When the snow was deep, neighbor boys shoveled and swept Mother's walk. She baked cookies to thank them.

Her new friends across the street, Jim and Linda, invited her to drinks or supper almost every week. Linda shared the latest fiction and biographies from the bookstore where she worked.

IN NOVEMBER, A year before Martin's accident, Tom and I were driving home from the airport after a trip to visit Sarah and Martin in the east. We hit a patch of icy slush. Our car rolled. Tom was all right. X-rays showed no breaks in my wrist, elbow, or shoulder, the places that hurt. We were both shaken, but not seriously injured.

Mother waited until after Christmas to tell me what had happened to her a few nights after our accident. She went into her garage to get wood to build a fire, something she did every winter evening. A man jumped out of the shadows, grabbed her, and tried to tear off her clothes. When she managed to scream, he ran away. She telephoned Jim and Linda, who called the police and brought her to their house for the night.

Because of our recent car accident, Mother decided not to tell us about her attack. When she did tell me, Sarah and Martin were out with friends, Tom was reading in our bedroom, and she and I were sitting in the living room. I, my arm still aching from our rollover, held her to comfort her, rocking as we both cried.

Never again would she mother me as before.

A WEEK LATER, just after New Year's, when she had gone home to Colorado, Mother fell in her bathroom and couldn't get up. She crawled to the bedroom and pulled a blanket off the foot of her bed to keep herself warm. She could have pulled the telephone down to the floor, but never thought to dial 911. She did not want care from strangers. Because she knew her old friends went to bed early, she waited until dawn to call them.

At the hospital, doctors found nothing amiss. They sent Mother home.

I drove to Colorado. I had a deadbolt put in Mother's garage door, found a company to install an alarm system, and got a panic button for her to wear around her neck. I posted notes reminding her to set the alarm when she went out. I did what I could to keep her safe. I drove home.

I wanted to hire someone to care for her. Too far away to take care of all Mother's needs, I imagined finding a surrogate daughter for her.

I thought I could find an easy solution.

Cathy, Mother's neighbor who taught at the college, was patient with me as we talked long distance about the Jehovah's Witness women in her North Dakota hometown who looked after old people. We both knew Mother would dismiss a fundamentalist caretaker. Cathy must have been waiting for me to figure out that Mother needed not a caretaker or a surrogate, but me, her daughter.

What did I need?

A push.

THAT APRIL, TOM and I took Mother with us to Mexico for a holiday. Away from the safety of her home and ours, where she could put her hand on a familiar chair for balance, she could not conceal her shakiness. Holding her hands, we walked her into the ocean. She pushed away from us and swam with graceful strokes.

Then she said, "I want to stop, but I can't make my feet go down." I dove, took her ankles in my hands, and set her feet on the ocean floor. Tom and I walked her back to the beach and settled her in a chair. We swam away from shore to talk, but did not have any answers, only worries.

When we came home to Santa Fe, Mother stayed with us in Santa Fe for three weeks. Occasionally, she said, "I should go home."

Whenever I said, "Stay a while longer," she yielded. As Madeline knew in the book Mother read to me when I was little, *Something was not right.*

I arranged for her to spend a night at Ponce de Leon, a retirement rental facility in Santa Fe. The next day she said, "I felt like a little girl being left at camp." She did not like the place—too much glitz, she said. It reminded her of the nursing home my father had first gone to when he started losing his mind.

FOUR AND A half years after he fell off his bicycle onto his head, my father began having psychotic breaks. He thought my mother was keeping him prisoner. One day he smashed a wooden chair in sudden fury. She grabbed the keys, ran to the car, and drove to the police for help. She could no longer keep him at home.

The first nursing home Mother found for him was overdecorated and too bright. All show, no heart. Mother hated leaving him there.

Her friend from wartime London came to New York for a conference. They visited nursing homes together, and he, a surgeon who cared for many elderly patients, coached her, telling her what to look for, what questions to ask. She found another nursing home, older and less shiny, where the staff was helpful.

She wrote an essay, *Some Thoughts on Nursing Homes—the Bad News and the Good News*, hoping "to present some basic tips for those who find themselves in a similar situation."

I wonder—did she ever imagine using those tips to find a place for herself? Could she ever have thought that Tom and I might need to find a place for Martin?

Still, when I talk about looking for nursing care, I learn how many have wrestled with that task. And, when Tom and I tell stories of our encounters with various insults to the brain—chemical, traumatic, or just plain weird and inexplicable—we find a host of others who know this landscape. We're not alone.

MOTHER AND I visited another retirement community, El Castillo, two blocks from the Plaza, Santa Fe's heart. We had lunch with a man and four women—Swiss, Danish, English, and American. We explored the courtyard gardens and several apartments.

El Castillo guarantees care for its residents throughout their lives. Because end-of-life care is the costliest part of the arrangement, the administration only wants healthy old people. Tom and I held our breath when Mother went for her interview. Would she pass the audition?

Months later, Mother's new friends told me that, because she seemed so frail and lost when she arrived, they couldn't understand how she passed the screening. I knew how—she's tough. She spent World War II in London. When she faces hardships, she says, "I went through the Blitz." She does not accept limitations, and she hides any weakness. In her interview with the director of nursing, she would have shone.

Mother gave up her Colorado garden where she sat on summer mornings in her dressing gown and snapped faded blossoms from her flowers. She gave up the fireplace that kept her company many nights. She gave away her old gray cat.

LYING AT HOME with my fractured skull, I think of the plans I had for welcoming my mother to Santa Fe—dinners, walks, bouquets, tea parties, museum expeditions. I wonder if in some way I chose to fall rather than confront my clashing emotions about Mother's neediness and frailty.

Before he lost his mind, my father offered sympathy for what he saw in my future. He warned that he would die first, Mother would become difficult, and I would have to care for her alone.

I think I am not a good daughter. I am bitter that my father, whom I thought I understood, died first. I am angry that my mother is failing. I don't want to be reasonable and accept her decline. I wish she would tell me what it is like to grow old. I wish she would tell me what she thinks and feels about my father and about everyone else she has loved and lost. But Mother does not open herself to me, perhaps because she never opens herself. She does not answer my questions.

Life is tough, and we must behave well and help others, is what I have learned from her.

Despite all my abandoned plans, some good does come of my fractured skull. Because I am not there, other residents look out for Mother in her first weeks at El Castillo, asking after me and finding ways to make her feel at home. Two months later, when we are away caring for Martin, she has good neighbors. Though not as I had planned, her needs are met.

THERE IS STILL another odd family brain story.

When Martin was a senior in high school, I found Tom lying on the bathroom floor after breakfast. He had vomited into the toilet. "Give me a couple of minutes," he said, "and then I'll get up."

I helped him to a sitting position. He threw up again. I called our doctor's office. The nurse said, *Bring Tom in right away.*

Each time I tried to help him up from the bathroom floor, he begged for a few more minutes to pull himself together. When our friend Katy called to say hello, I told her he was sick and I didn't know what was wrong. She said she'd come right over. I said I could manage without help.

Lying on the floor, Tom told me he couldn't understand what he kept seeing—fantastically tall men dressed all in white, in a totally white room.

In our real life, dry wall installers had just smoothed all the textured walls and ceilings of a house we were renovating. Dressed in white, they covered the floors with white drop cloths and slathered every surface with white sheet rock compound. They walked on stilts to smooth the upper walls.

But Tom had no memory of the previous days, and he could make no sense of his surreal white visions.

And he wouldn't, or couldn't, get up. When I called a second time, the doctor's nurse said, *Call 911.* I did, and then called Katy back. She arrived as the medics were lifting Tom onto a gurney, and she followed the ambulance to the hospital.

He kept asking the medics who they were and, borrowing from grade B movies, threatened, "You're going to have a lot of explaining to do." Familiar with his ironic tone, I knew he knew that *he* was the one who would have a hard time explaining what was going on.

In the emergency room, Tom could not remember what day or month it was. But when the doctor said it was December eighth, Tom responded, "A day that will live in infamy. Or was that yesterday?"

When the doctor asked him the time, Tom looked at the doctor's watch and told the time. A minute later, the doctor asked the time again, covering his watch with his hand. Tom sneaked a look at the clock on the wall. A minute later, when the doctor covered his watch and I blocked the view of the wall clock, Tom had no idea what time it was.

Tom knew that Clinton was the president, and added, "He's not living up to our hopes."

When a nurse asked him his name, Tom answered, "Fritz."

"Last name?" the nurse continued, filling out forms. I knew Tom would answer, "the Cat."

"She thinks you're serious," I told him. "Give her your real name."

I kept explaining Tom's cryptic comments to the nurse and

doctor. His short-term memory was gone, but his intellect was fine. His sense of humor and his feistiness confused everyone but me. To me, they were proof that Tom was still himself. For him, they helped mask his helplessness.

After the doctor ordered a CT, no one came to take Tom for the scan. Finally, Katy left our curtained space. She went to the nurses' station and insisted they call the technicians to tell them Tom was ready for his scan.

Katy pushed, and things that needed to happen got done. I learned from her that there should always be two people with a patient—one for company and love, and a second as the patient's advocate.

Tom's scan showed nothing medically amiss, no sign of a clot or stroke. A nurse gave him an anti-nausea injection. Almost immediately, his nausea went away. A minute later, he became intensely agitated. Over and over he said, "If I can just look out a window, I'll be fine." He tried to climb off the high gurney. He cursed the hospital's lack of windows. He repeated the local rumor that Santa Fe's hospital had been built from plans bought on the cheap after another city rejected them. A nurse gave him an anti-anxiety injection and he calmed down.

After five hours, we brought Tom home. Lying in bed, he asked me over and over what had happened. He had no memory of the morning or of the hospital. When I told him that medics had wheeled him out of our house on a gurney, he did not believe me. Only when I got him up and showed him the gurney's tracks in the carpet did he stop saying, "You're making this up." The episode of *transient global amnesia* was over.

Transient global amnesia is a sudden, temporary period of memory loss than can't be attributed to a more common neurological condition. One cannot recall events, nor, sometimes, things that happened a day or a month or a year ago. After the incident, the patient remembers nothing of the episode and, occasionally, nothing of the hours before. Otherwise, his memory is fine.

Two days later, a neurologist reviewed Tom's CT scans and said he had had an ischemic attack, the blood supply to his brain had been interrupted, he didn't know why, and it was unlikely to happen again.

Tom told me what he had learned: *Only the thinnest thread keeps us connected to the world we know.*

I, too, had learned something. The moment I realized that my husband, lying on our bathroom floor, did not know what was going on, I thought of the years my mother had lived with my father's dementia. I knew that I would care for Tom as long as he needed me, and I saw my mother and father in a new light.

I never imagined what could happen less than three years later, when our family learned even more about what mishaps can befall the brain. I never dreamed how much more we would learn about care and commitment.

The Environment Crashing In:
Neurological Ward

The eye of man hath not heard, the ear of man hath not seen,
man's hand is not able to taste, his tongue to conceive, nor his
heart to report, what my dream was.

William Shakespeare, *A Midsummer Night's Dream*

MOST OF OUR LIVES, we exist in a present that has a familiar frame of reference, guided by similar events that have happened to us or to others we know. Outcomes are predictable.

In a hospital's ICU, you have no frame of reference, because you don't have your or others' similar circumstances to guide you. At most, you walk past the door of a room where someone you met in the waiting room stands beside a bed, and you guess that the patient is someone whose story you heard.

You have no sense of the future, and the present is a bewildering fog. You accept that your task is simply to *Be Here Now*. *Be Here Now* is a book written by a spiritual teacher who calls himself Ram

Dass. It has been in my bedside cabinet since the Sixties. I don't look at it much, but it is there now.

Later, Tom reflects on our first weeks after Martin's accident: "Dealing with the constant issues of the present was good, in a way. We didn't have to face the big questions. That's one way we got through it. There was enough going on. We were not able to dwell on our fears."

ON TUESDAY EVENING, a week after Martin's accident, a nurse tells us that our son, after a week in the ICU, is being transferred to the neurology ward. Although no fanfare marks his passage from extreme danger to what everyone hopes will be a journey of recovery, we know it is momentous.

Dr. Mustapha Ezzedine comes into Martin's room. He says he will miss hearing Miles Davis as he walks by. There is a joyful light in his green eyes because Martin is well enough to be moved out of Intensive Care. Dr. Ezzedine, a resident, not a full-fledged neurologist, seems to live the ICU, just as we do. No one else comments on our departure.

We are learning that an elaborate class system exists at Mass General. It seems so Bostonian, where *the Lowells speak only to the Cabots and the Cabots speak only to God.* God is the neurosurgeon, Dr. Hammer, and He speaks to us only because Harvard University Health Services' Director interceded on our behalf. God speaks tersely, in an arcane language we struggle to understand. He does not meet our eyes. He never has more than a minute for us.

In the hierarchy of medical specialties, neurosurgery is at the top, cardiology somewhat lower, orthopedics lower still, and trauma below orthopedics. Doctors rank above nurses, although to us no one is more heroic than the nurses. Tom and I love them for all they interpret for us. They explain why the neurosurgeon wants Martin's intracranial pressure to go down before he removes the drain from his head and why the orthopedist ordered certain tests.

The hierarchy continues below the lofty realm of doctors. ICU nurses outrank respiratory and speech therapists, who in turn come in above the technicians who draw blood. Below ICU nurses are ward nurses. Below them come the nursing aides who wash patients and change their clothes and bedding.

The first aide we meet is a large Samoan man, for whom lifting skinny Martin is nothing at all. Although he is gentle, we assume his work takes strength, not skill. Then we meet a tiny Thai aide. She does the same work as the big man, and we realize that skill, not size, is the force empowering the aides.

As you go down the medical hierarchy, there are shifts in gender and language. Most doctors are male. Most nurses are female. Doctors speak Standard English or are immigrants, learning Standard English. Nurses often have a strong Boston accent.

A few ICU nurses act put out that Tom and I are in Martin's room so much of the time, and stridently assert their rules. Privately, Tom calls them "nurse Nazis." Several are so ferociously competent that Tom and I speculate that, had they been born middle-class males, they would be neurosurgeons.

Many aides speak English poorly, although one, whom I dislike for her roughness with Martin, is an older white woman. I wonder if she resents working as a nursing aide, a job now done by many immigrants. When she is on duty, I do everything I can do for

Martin myself, so she will have no chance to handle him roughly.

Some workers who mop the floors or empty the waste receptacles speak no English—just Spanish, or Portuguese, or Haitian Creole. But Maria, whose first language is Portuguese, speaks Spanish with Martin and English with me.

We, the patient's family, are close to the bottom of the hierarchy. Some nurses act as if we are disturbing them. Nonetheless, they tolerate our being with Martin.

Martin is so deep in the valley of the shadow, I believe that he needs us to help him find his way back to life. To come back, he needs skilled care from the doctors and nurses, and, from us, words and songs, hands touching him, and love. We must make sure that everyone accepts our staying beside him.

MARTIN HAD A room to himself in the ICU and only family members were allowed in to see him. The ICU receptionist screened each visitor before she unlocked the door to the unit. The neurological ward's double entry doors are always propped open. Anyone may visit.

We invite our friend Katy's daughter to meet us in the ICU waiting room. Aurora has known Martin all his life. Now twenty-four, a radiant woman with her mother's dark hair and flashing eyes, she is in Boston for a week. She arrives just as Martin is being moved from the ICU, and walks alongside as they wheel him to the ward. His eyes are shut tight.

Like her mother, Aurora is intensely present. Moments after meeting Katy, someone once said, "It's like she swallowed uranium. She glows in the dark." So does her daughter.

Aurora has friends who suffered terrible traumas. One was hit by a train, the other hurt in a car accident. One is doing well, the other is not. Aurora has been at bedsides like Martin's before. She knows, perhaps better than we, that the outcome cannot be guessed.

IN HIS NEW bed in the ward, Martin lies with his eyes still shut tight. Aurora takes his hand and says, "Hello my darling Martin, it's Aurora."

He opens his eyes and exclaims, "Auroraburger!"

She has never heard our silly name for her. She giggles.

Because Clint and Aurora are like family, and because both have been with brain-injured patients before, we welcome their visits. But because Martin is likely to become agitated, we do not let his college friends see him in the ward. We don't want them to take away images that will be painful for them or embarrassing for him later on. We hope that Martin will get better and we think he would not want his friends to have seen him loud and angry, yelling obscenities.

Perhaps that is a bad decision. His friends should understand, and they might hasten his recovery. We are so immersed in the present, with no time for *should* and *might*, we follow our intuition. Like the doctors, we may make mistakes.

IN THE WARD, no one at the nursing station even looks up as we walk by, and we hardly see any doctors. There are two patients in every room, and a single nurse cares for six. After spending a week in the ICU's cocoon, we find the ward terrifying.

Martin's ward nurse, Lynette DiAngelo, moves faster than any nurse we have seen, and she is totally tuned into all Martin's needs. Tom and I love her name—she is our gift from the angels.

The ward is strict only in its rule that visitors must leave by nine o'clock. After Martin's first night in the ward, we arrive early. He is alone in the room. The other bed is empty. Lynette says Martin shouted and cursed so loudly, the night nurses moved his roommate to another room.

The second night, the same thing happens with a different roommate.

One doctor tells us, "The environment crashing in after a comatose state can be very agitating. Mania, obsession, bad language— all are standard."

The nurses agree that Martin's manic behavior is normal for someone recovering from brain injury.

We have gotten over so many hurdles—getting Martin to move his fingers and his toes, taking him off the ventilator, getting him to eat, removing the tube from his brain, getting him out of Intensive Care—and now he is shouting and cursing, acting crazy. Tom is afraid that Martin's progress may have come to an end, that he may stay like this, loud and angry and unreasonable.

I do not consider this possibility. Katy has written us about this phase. Ten years ago her son's friend skied into a tree; she described for us the wild stage he went through. The friend's mother writes to us too, offering to talk with us about the difficult path to recovery, a path she knows well.

I ALSO REMEMBER my father's voluble craziness right after his first operation. Then, in the week that followed, more fluid accumulated inside his brain and he became silent. The doctor reopened his skull and drained the fluid off again. After his second operation, Daddy was not wild, only mute. After almost a week, he spoke his first words.

"What are my chances of survival?" he asked.

"You have survived," Mother answered.

"*J'ai survecu?*" he asked in French. *I survived?* "Like Talleyrand?"

"*Tu as survecu,*" she assured him. "You have survived."

Daddy was quoting a French statesman who lived through the Revolution and beyond. My father's power of speech had come back and, with it, evidence of his complex intellect.

Four and a half years later, Daddy became demented and dangerous. Mother could not care for him at home. She visited him every day in the nursing home.

I hope that Martin will recover and I know that if he does not, I will care for him.

MARTIN'S THIRD ROOMMATE is Larry, a brick mason. He has had a tumor removed from his brain. No one visits Larry, and we are polite but distant, worried about the difficult night we know lies ahead for him.

The next morning, Larry is still in the room. We ask if Martin gave him a rough night.

"No," he says, "but he seemed a bit upset. So I asked him about his family." Larry has learned that we live in New Mexico, and he knows that Martin's sister Sarah works for BBC television in New York. He has kept Martin calm by getting him to talk about the people he loves. Larry is our new hero, a kind and wise man.

THE BRAIN TRAUMA has damaged his thirst regulator and Martin is always thirsty. Worried that liquids will increase the swelling in his brain, the doctors insist on keeping his fluid intake to a careful minimum, and on measuring every ounce he drinks.

Every time a nurse raises the permitted milliliters on the white board above Martin's bed, we rejoice. But the increase is never enough and Martin is thirsty all the time. He calls his favorite drink—ginger ale and cranberry juice—"the Nectar of the Gods." Larry, impressed, asks where he learned that phrase. Martin answers, "Shakespeare, I think."

Determined and wily, he reaches weakly for the cup we offer, then holds it fiercely and drains every drop. We learn to pour an ounce at a time so he cannot drink too much.

Tom has hated every minute that Martin had to suffer the ET tube down his windpipe. Now he can't bear Martin's thirst. He says, "My life revolves around trying to cope with Martin's thirst. Can I get five more minutes before I have to start arguing with him?"

Exhausted after arguing with me for more liquid, Martin cries out, "You're supposed to be on my side."

"I *am* on your side," I say firmly.

Martin says, "This is my greatest opus. Climbing's not this hard. But close."

His lips dry out and blister. I smooth vitamin E oil on them and massage the oil on the scars on his head and forehead.

I worry at how Tom cheats a little, but I too can't keep from giving Martin sips of water and slipping tiny ice chips into his mouth. We give him applesauce to soothe his thirst.

Martin reasons, "If applesauce, with its high water content, is unrestricted, why not water?" It's a question I can't answer. Tom wonders whether the body takes up water in food differently from water in liquid form. I doubt his logic, and just tell Martin that the doctors are concerned that too much liquid in his system may increase his intracranial pressure. Martin is loud and angry, just as Katy warned he would be. "Doctors, schmoctors," he says. Later, he elaborates, "Doctors don't know shit."

ONE EVENING WHEN he was in high school, Martin announced that his English teacher was ill and would not be back for months.

"Who's the substitute?" I asked.

"Mr. Garcia," Martin said.

In a robotic monotone I asked, "Do – you – mean – the – Mr. – Garcia – who – talks – like – this?"

"You know him!" said Martin.

I feared that Martin, along with some 140 other students, would waste much of his junior year with a poor substitute teacher. I had taught high school English for several years before Sarah was born, and later, when both children were in school, as a long term substitute teacher. I persuaded the high school to give me the job until the regular English teacher returned.

One student came alive in class only when he gave a report on the poem he had chosen, Allen Ginsberg's *Howl*. I was considering how to deal with his coarse language without smothering his passion when another student spoke from across the room.

"Luke," she said, "you could be so much more eloquent."

From my notebook:

> . . . *I remind Martin when he swears that he "could be so much more—"*
>
> *"Eloquent," he fills in. The nurse is astonished.*
>
> *Last night I was leaving. Martin was agitated, upset, swearing, sweating. I stroked his head where the hair is getting shaggy. He quieted a little. Then I lay on him, bent from the waist, my heart crosswise on his, and breathed slowly, constantly murmuring slower and slower for him to breathe slowly, to breathe with my breathing, to beat with my heart. His inhalations deepened, his breathing and heartbeats slowed, and he was quiet, and he slept.*
>
> *This morning I sit looking upriver. The T slides over the Charles. I count its cars, six. Trees are turning browns and reds and yellows, nothing brilliant, but soft colors. The cosmos are blooming six feet off the ground. No freeze yet.*
>
> *It's 8:30 and the doctors haven't rounded yet, or the nurse missed seeing them. Sunday. The T crosses the river. A bus crosses on the farther bridge. I must be looking southwest, from the way the light slants.*
>
> *I don't like writing on the left-hand page so I don't. It can be so easy figuring out what to do. Food is important— just fuel to keep going—or it's wonderful, strawberry cream*

cheese on a bagel or spinach ravioli in a spinach sauce.
Martin sleeps. I wish I could sing.

Settling into waiting, while Martin sets the pace, for a moment I am almost happy.

Suppertime, and Tom is with Martin. I walk to the subway at Charles Street where the train comes up to cross the river on its way to Cambridge. I wait at the end of the platform out on the bridge, watching the sun set golden up the river. From the Central Square stop, I walk to Clint's. I make calls, scramble eggs, and sleep.

A WEEK AND a half after the accident, Dr. Altman stops by the neurological ward. A neurologist Clint sometimes consults, Dr. Altman has visited before. We tell him that Martin reacted badly to Haldol, an anti-psychotic drug, and spiked a high fever. They have stopped giving him Haldol.

Altman is furious. He says that there is no need for an anti-psychotic drug; that Martin's intense agitation is standard after brain injury; that there is no psychosis; and that Haldol is notoriously dangerous for young men. Then he sees the air pressure boots they put on Martin's legs in the ICU. He peels apart the Velcro holding them in place and looks at his bruised legs. Martin thrashes about.

"Those are designed to prevent clotting in immobile patients, and Martin hasn't been still for a moment since I came in," Altman says. He throws the boots under the bed.

"Treat the patient," Martin's EMT instructor told her students. I wonder, *Have Martin's doctors been so deep in their textbooks that they have forgotten to look at him?* Tom blames himself for letting Martin's bruises get worse for so many days. And no one ever suggests using the boots again.

Laughter, Fear, and the Rich Smell of Earth

Nothing would give up life:
Even the dirt kept breathing a small breath.

Theodore Roethke, "Root Cellar"

A FEW CARDS AND LETTERS arrive for Martin at Mass General, but during our first week there, we forget that he has a mailbox back at Lowell House. After he moves to the ward, Tom asks if he remembers the combination.

"I do," he answers.

"I'll go get the mail for you," Tom says. "Can you tell me the combination?"

"I can," Martin says, "but then I'd have to kill you."

It is his first joke since the accident. We think it a significant milestone in his recovery, a sign of his mental sharpness, but know we may be setting too great store by trivial events, hoping for hope.

The speech therapist comes by. She no longer has to weigh the dangers of feeding her patient by mouth and focuses instead on his thinking. She asks Martin simple questions—his name, where he goes to school, who the president is. He gets the answers right, but he does not know his age or what month it is. He can count backward from one hundred by sevens. Then she gives him more arithmetic problems.

"You go to an appointment that will last two hours. You park your car at a meter that gives you half an hour for each dime. How much money should you put into the meter?"

Martin asks her, "What does the meter max out at?"

Whenever we visited our friend, Josefina, at her café the week before the accident, Tom kept going out to feed the meter. It always maxed out at something less than the time we needed. When we lost track of time and fed it late, we found a ticket on our windshield. Tom grumbled how he hated parking around Harvard Square.

Martin has never liked arithmetic, and he has a terrible headache. By asking "What does the meter max out at?" he has both ducked doing arithmetic and gotten a laugh.

The next day Dr. Woo comes by the hospital. A friend of a friend, she was the neurological unit administrator at Spaulding Rehabilitation Hospital several years ago. We tell her about Martin joking he'd have to kill Tom if he gave him the mailbox's combination and about his dodging the parking meter problem.

She says, "He is showing the kind of higher thinking that can't be taught. Arithmetic is a lesser skill. He can relearn it easily if he needs to."

Tom and I retell Martin's clever answers when friends call for news. We try to explain how enormously promising his comebacks are, and how they show that his thought processes are subtle and complex. Our friends don't challenge us, but they probably can't understand why we are so pleased. They don't know how far Martin has already come.

WE REMEMBER MARTIN'S cleverness as a little boy. He had a gift for the limelight, and for mischief. We toured the Queen Mary in Long Beach when Sarah was ten and he was eight. When we walked into the grand ballroom near the end of a magic show, a child from the audience was assisting, passing cardboard blocks to the magician. The magician was leaning back, his eyes on the ceiling. The child passed each block to him, and he balanced the blocks on his forehead, making a tower.

We watched to the end of the show and stayed for the next performance. When, at last, the magician asked for a child volunteer to help him, Martin's hand shot up. The magician chose our little boy with the freckles, the shaggy haircut, and the innocent smile.

On stage, Martin stood quiet and obedient until the magician had two cardboard blocks balanced on his forehead. Martin was to hand him the blocks, one at a time. He held the next block out, just two inches beyond the man's reach. The magician, his eyes on the ceiling, groped for the block as Martin smiled in the spotlight, pretending to be oblivious to his not being able to grasp the block. The audience laughed. The magician, suddenly the straight man, groped for each block until Martin chose to put it in his hand. Trusting in a child's desire to win approval, the magician assumed he'd picked a boy who was either slow-witted or too dazzled by the lights to remember his assignment.

Martin was indeed dazzled by the lights, and he chose to be the star comedian. Tom and Sarah and I, hoping no one would know we had brought the child who was stealing the show, tried not to laugh louder than the rest of the audience.

MARTIN DUCKS SOME of the speech therapist's other questions. He answers one with a request for more details. Trying to get her off track saves him from having to solve problems.

Later, Tom points out to me that, because Martin is color blind, he learned alternative strategies for problem solving at an early age.

At four, he came to me with a red crayon and a green crayon. He asked which was red. I thought he was teasing. Playing along, I took the red crayon and showed him the word on the paper, R-E-D. Then I showed him G-R-E-E-N on the other crayon and pointed out that *green* was a longer word than *red*, so he could always tell the words apart.

Soon after that, an ophthalmologist tested the children in his preschool. Martin was red/green color blind.

I started playing the *Beep Beep* game with Sarah and Martin— when you see a yellow VW beetle, the first person to say "Beep yellow" earns a point. We saw beep blues, beep oranges, beep blacks, beep whites. Martin resisted talking about how he saw colors, but his color vocabulary expanded and I learned that he could not tell magenta (blue mixed with red) from deep turquoise (blue mixed with green).

Martin figured out unknown colors in I way that I thought was like solving an algebra problem. Knowing which shirt we called red, he could put it beside a color he did not know and which, because he could tell most other colors, he guessed was either red or green. If what it did to his eyes was similar to what the known red shirt did, he guessed that the unknown color was also red. If it did something different, he guessed it was green.

Martin's talent for what Dr. Woo calls *higher thinking skills* and Tom describes as *alternative strategies for problem solving*, was helped by his color-blindness, something others see as a disability. That talent will become a powerful ally as he puts the pieces of himself and his life together again.

MARTIN'S THIRST SENSOR is still out of whack, or perhaps he just needs more liquids than the doctors allow. After the artifactual ICP readings, after the anti-psychotic drug he reacted to so badly, after the pressure boots that bruised his thrashing legs, and after hearing that he *was, wasn't, was* in a coma, we no longer believe the doctors know everything. We begin to pay greater attention to our own insights, but we are still frightened by how much we don't know, and by how little experience we have in this new territory.

Perhaps the doctors' fluid restrictions are excessive or even unnecessary, but we try to follow them, giving Martin only a sip when he is thirsty.

Martin's sense of needing to pee is also confused. He asks for the urinal every few minutes. Remembering Maria, the Portuguese woman who spoke Spanish with him in the ICU, he says he wants to know how to say *I want to pee* in Portuguese. Maria is not around, but Aurora was an exchange student in Brazil. She teaches Martin to say, *Eu preciso fazer chi chi.*

Martin learns fast. In the wild manner that we have learned is typical for those recovering from brain injury, he declaims that he will pee for the sake of all the Portuguese people, and also for the sake of the people of Brazil. We laugh until our sides hurt.

It is the first time that he has heard us laugh since his accident. With his mother and father laughing so hard, he must feel safe.

AT NIGHT, I return calls from New Mexico, where it is two hours earlier. I talk with a Jungian analyst whose son and Martin were high school friends. Jerome worries that Martin will need a gifted psychiatrist to guide him as he re-enters his life. He tells me that psychiatry has moved away from emotional and spiritual therapy. Psychiatrists now are trained as pharmacists. They do not have the training and do not take the time to care for the wounded spirit. "A trauma like this can be very destabilizing."

Jerome's warnings echo through the days that follow. I imagine emotional breakdowns, I imagine Martin unable to fit what he has experienced into his life after the accident, and I imagine him stuck, unable to get beyond some point in his recovery because his psyche is unsteady.

Months and years later, I still hear Jerome's words. I wonder if, overwhelmed by Martin's immediate needs and the logistics of attending to them, I have been careless, not adequately concerned. And then I am gentle with myself and remember that I kept Jerome's warning as a constant reminder to be alert to any sign of Martin becoming distressed. And then, frightened again, I wonder if I was perceptive enough.

THE ICU NURSES have told us that Martin will not be able to go home until he has spent weeks or months in a rehabilitation hospital. They brush off our questions about what his rehabilitation will involve. With no idea of what to look for, we set out to assess the possible hospitals. We'll find out what we need to know as we go.

Dr. Woo and all the Mass General doctors recommend

Spaulding Rehabilitation Hospital. On Wednesday, the day after Martin is moved to the ward, we walk out a back door of Mass General, across a one-way street, over a lawn, past apartments (*We could rent one*, we think), alongside a construction site, and across another street.

We take the elevator to the twelfth floor. The building branches into two wings—the adult neurological unit and the pediatric neurological unit. We thread our way down the adult wing's corridor past patients practicing using their wheelchairs. They look lost and broken. Tom and I walk back to the elevators. We hold each other. I blink back tears. Everyone here is so damaged, unhappy, alone.

After we visit the children's wing, we decide that we will do anything to have Martin, who has six months before his twenty-first birthday, spend his rehabilitation among children. He loved working with children in a day camp last summer. We imagine that he can help the children here, and that being around them will give both him and us hope. But even Spaulding's pediatric unit is dispiriting. It is close to the bleak adult wing, and it is crowded, chaotic, too hot, too bright, too high above the ground.

That afternoon, we drive to Youville Rehabilitation Hospital in Cambridge, near Harvard. "Martin's friends can visit easily," we reassure each other. The basement is set up with a replica of a post office complete with stamps and a scale for letters, a little beauty parlor with brushes and combs, a mini-grocery with shopping baskets, and a pretend bank. It reminds me of *Sesame Street*. We think that Martin is past needing such a place, and would find it condescending.

Although he cannot sit up, Martin does not need such facsimiles of life. He knows that applesauce is full of water, remembers his mailbox combination, and understands the limits of parking meters.

Youville's grounds are green and its buildings low and pleasant, but it is too quiet and too cold, with no one in its halls or in the basement's pretend village. We will keep looking.

The next day we drive to Braintree, several traffic jams south of Boston. Tom is not patient in traffic. Sarah and Martin and I sometimes say, "One red light can ruin his whole day."

Braintree Rehabilitation Hospital is less chaotic than Spaulding and livelier than Youville, neither too hot nor too cold. We like the therapists and doctors we meet. Dr. Woo has said good things about the chief neuro-physiatrist. (A physiatrist is a doctor who specializes in rehabilitation.) Martin could go outside into the lovely small garden area. But it is an ordeal for us driving back to Boston with all the traffic.

Martin's ward nurse takes us aside. "Check out New England Rehab in Woburn," she says, "and don't tell anyone I told you."

Dr. Altman stops by. He says the same thing: "Check out New England Rehab in Woburn."

On Friday, we drive half an hour north, to Woburn. Coming up the long driveway, Tom says, "I've been here."

I first think he is speaking metaphorically, that to him the place feels familiar and right.

It is not a metaphor. Ten years earlier, he drove his mother out to Woburn. They looked at the retirement apartments we pass as we drive up the hill to the hospital.

"This is the place," Tom says. "I'm sure."

A pale young man sits in a wheelchair behind the front desk. We lean forward to hear him better. He tells us he was once a patient here and now he works part-time at the desk.

The woman we arranged our visit with on the phone takes us to the third, top floor of the building. A huge skylight floods a central atrium with light. The atrium is open to the floors below, with railings around the open space. Two patients use the railings as exercise bars, lifting their legs or hopping on one foot, while others walk slowly through the bright hallways. One or two therapists accompany each patient.

The south wing off the atrium is for brain rehabilitation—for patients who have had strokes, tumors, or traumatic brain injury. The head nurse shows us the double rooms along the corridors, and then the corner rooms with four beds.

"Martin," she says, "will not be in a corner room, because it is important not to over-stimulate patients with traumatic brain injury."

The neuro-physiatrist joins us. With her pale complexion, fine hair, and alert eyes, Dr. Sandra Suduikis makes me think of a clever rabbit. We pause in our conversation as children from the daycare center downstairs prance through the corridor wearing Halloween costumes. Dr. Suduikis's daughter and the nurse's three-year-old are among them.

Below the hospital to the east are woods and a lake. To the west are the retirement apartments, woods, and a golf course. This seems the right place for Martin, a refuge in the country. Nurses and doctors have been telling us to move him out of Mass General as soon as we can. They say he will not start to get better until then.

Tom and I reassure each other that, if we are wrong about New England Rehab, we can always move Martin again. We think this place on the hill is right for the next phase of his recovery. We hope he will start to get well here.

Until now, we have been following others' leads, moving out of their way, obeying restrictions we don't understand, accepting doctors ignoring us, and grateful when Dr. Coley gets them to talk with us. Choosing a rehab hospital is the first significant step we have taken on our own.

AURORA'S LAST DAY in Boston is Saturday, Halloween. Sarah is in Boston too, so we invite both young women to spend that night with us at Clint's. Relieved that we have chosen a rehabilitation hospital, I stay up late with Aurora and Sarah, as we did when they were little girls and Aurora's mother was part of our sleepover party.

In New York, Sarah's colleagues have arranged their schedules so she can come to Boston every Friday afternoon. On our second Sunday morning, after our slumber party with Aurora, Sarah and I walk to the Central Square subway together. In New York, just a few days ago, we had talked about troubles she was having with some of her friends. I ask her whether, since Martin's accident, anything has changed. She answers, "*Everything* has changed, Mom."

IT TAKES FROM Friday until Tuesday to move Martin to New England Rehabilitation Hospital. There are phone calls among nurses, social workers, and administrators, plus masses of paperwork for them all to fill out. Nothing happens over the weekend; in their worlds, Saturdays and Sundays don't count. For us, every day matters.

On Tuesday, without warning, two medics appear in Martin's room. They lift him onto their gurney and wrap him in blankets. Tom has left to rent the car we will need in Woburn. I stuff Martin's few belongings and dozens of get well cards into plastic bags. The medics load the gurney's baskets with all his flowers.

As when we moved him from the ICU, Martin appears to be asleep. Maybe this is his way of protecting himself from chaos.

The medics make everyone else get off the elevator and take us straight to the ground floor, ten stories down. Martin has already moved from the silence of the ICU to the bustling ward, but traveling on a gurney is even wilder than being in the ward. As the medics speed him through the hallways to the elevator and out to the waiting ambulance, his senses are assaulted by shifting light, temperature changes, different smells, wind, noise, and uneven pavement. He gives no sign of consciousness.

In the ambulance, one medic sits beside Martin, taking his pulse and blood pressure every few minutes. I sit by his head, my hands on his shoulders. I remember the pain of my ride to the Santa Fe hospital when I fractured my skull. In that ambulance, I was on the gurney, and Martin sat by my head. Then, he was saving me.

We pass Spaulding. "Almost everyone at Mass General wanted us to go there," I say.

The medic says, "We take a lot of patients there, and we bring a lot of them back to Mass General a week later because of infections they get at Spaulding."

Martin does not stir or open his eyes in the ambulance. When we arrive at the top of the Woburn hill and the medics pull the gurney out of the ambulance, I say to him, "Look up! There are trees, and clouds, and sky."

He does not show that he hears me. He does not open his eyes. I hope we are doing the right thing, bringing him here. The air smells fresh and damp, of leaves and earth.

I REMEMBER THE morning I first saw my father after his head injury. My parents' friends, Sherry and Bob, picked me and my baby up at the airport and drove us to their house. I left Sarah with Sherry, and Bob drove me to the hospital. On the back stairs to the ICU, where the sweet disinfectant couldn't cover the sour smell of illness, I met my father's doctor. His mannerisms were so formal and awkward, for a moment I wondered if he was trying to make me laugh. He was the doctor who had sent my father home a week earlier, giving my mother no guidance about signs to watch for that could mean trouble.

My father's eyes looked huge beneath his bandaged head. They opened wide as I came in, and he told the man beside him, a handsome young Episcopal priest, "This is my daughter. She came from New Mexico." He said nothing more.

They let me stay ten minutes. I was relieved to walk away from the whiteness of sheets and bandages and the sharp disinfectant smell.

My father loved gardening. In the spring and summer, he came home from work in the evening. "Let's go make the rounds," he'd say. We walked outside to see which plant had pushed through the earth that day, how many buds had opened, whether any fruit was ripe. When I was small, my job was to crawl under bushes to pick up pieces of paper that had blown there. In August, Daddy took baskets of bright zinnias and ripe tomatoes to his office to give away. When the Peace Rose was introduced in the early 1950's, he thought its cream and peach colored blossoms exquisite. Because he had been a soldier, the Peace

Rose's name pleased him. Because Daddy had no sense of smell, he asked me to describe the new rose's scent. Every winter, he pored over the seed catalog, dreaming of his summer garden. He loved finding new sources for manure, and he loved debating with other gardeners the merits of horse versus chicken fertilizer.

While my father lay in the ICU, Mother helped Sherry in the kitchen, and my baby slept. I sat on the patio watching Bob dig manure into the garden, getting ready to plant. Nothing ever smelled so good as that earth in the February sunshine, not until the damp leafy air on the hill above the Woburn lake.

Above the Woods:
New England Rehabilitation Hospital, Part 1

Try to remember this: what you project
Is what you will perceive; what you perceive
With any passion, be it love or terror,
May take on whims and powers of its own.

Richard Wilbur, "Walking to Sleep"

A T NEW ENGLAND REHAB, Martin's room faces east, overlooking trees and Horn Pond far below. A girl brings papers to the room for me to sign. She looks frightened. Martin is the first patient she has helped admit who is almost as young as she.

Both beds are empty. We put Martin in the one by the window and fill the room with his flowers and cards. We tape up a photo of him taken a week before his accident, goofing around with someone's electric drill and grinning. I want everyone at New England Rehab to imagine the wonderful Martin they haven't yet come to know, so they can help him recover the joy he has lost.

Outside the window, an oak tree glistens after rain and catches the light of sunrise every morning. At dusk we say *Good night* to the oak before we pull the curtains, hoping that soon Martin will stand beside us for the evening ritual.

TOM AND I are accustomed to giving support to others and to doing things for ourselves. In our changed circumstances, we find ourselves accepting offers of help from our friends. We are astonished at all the ways the word of Martin's accident has spread: through grocery store encounters, church bulletins, telephone, e-mail. We get help with our tenants' plumbing problems and our real estate business. Sarah's friends arrange to continue feeding our cats and watering our plants. We concentrate on taking care of Martin.

WITH DAILY CONTACT and shared staff, Harvard Medical School, Massachusetts General Hospital, and Spaulding Rehab are so intertwined that almost everyone connected with one of them believes the other two to be the best. When Tom or I asked for advice about rehab hospitals, almost everyone assumed we would choose Spaulding.

Just half an hour north of Boston, New England Rehabilitation Hospital is another world. Rank seems of little importance, and patients' needs are paramount. Nurses and aides make suggestions with confidence. Doctors listen to nurses and the nurses respect the doctors. We, the patient's family, are partners in his recovery.

Dr. Suduikis, Martin's neuro-physiatrist and lead physician, says Martin probably will need six to eight weeks of rehabilitation before he can travel home to New Mexico. We expect to be in Woburn past the New Year.

THE FIRST NIGHT at New England Rehab, Martin's nurse tells us that patients do better when they wear their own clothes. At Mass General, we threw away the jeans, belt, shirt, and jacket the paramedics had cut off him. We kept his socks and his one boot. Without much logic or perspective, I called the ambulance company and the police to see if they had the other boot. They didn't.

Martin arrived at New England Rehab wearing a blue and white cotton hospital gown from Mass General. When he falls asleep, Tom and I drive to a mall nearby. We buy sweat pants and light-weight drawstring pants, a soft long sleeved shirt with a loose neck opening that will be easy to pull over his head, and warm slippers with traction soles. A few days later, Tom goes to Martin's college room and brings back his running shoes, flamboyant red lounge pants, shirts, jeans, socks, and underwear. Martin, over six feet tall, has dropped below 120 pounds. His jeans, always loose, now flap around his body.

When we began our trip a month earlier, I had brought no winter clothing. I have been wearing some of Martin's shirts and sweaters to keep warm. I love the Harvard Ultimate Frisbee team sweatshirt that Martin wore when he could run and play. Now I give it back to him.

AT MASS GENERAL, the nurses tied Martin's hands to the bed rails to keep him from hurting himself. Now, in Woburn, he is still intensely agitated and still swearing. Still thrashing to get up, he is too weak to stand up safely without help. A nurse tells us that last month a patient fell, hit his head, and was taken back to the hospital he had just left, for more brain surgery. We are terrified.

The nurses remind us that agitation is normal after traumatic brain injury. One recommends a special bed, a canopied enclosure that surrounds the regular hospital bed. It arrives the next day. Its top and sides are made of a coarse white mesh that looks like netting to keep out huge mosquitoes. Whenever we go out of the room, even for a minute, we zip Martin in so he can't fall out.

The Harvard men's and women's Ultimate Frisbee teams have sent Frisbees covered with hand-written get well wishes and messages of love. We put the Frisbees on top of the netting along with Martin's favorite *Sesame Street* muppet. Furry blue Grover, my gift to Martin earlier in the year, was peeking out of his backpack when we picked him up at the airport last June. Grover went back to college with him in September.

Martin eventually will learn to unzip the bed enclosure from the inside. By then he will understand how vulnerable he is and how serious falling and hitting his head would be, and he will not try to climb out alone. Meanwhile, he is free from the restraints Mass General used to keep him safe. He can turn from side to side and thrash about without hurting himself. Over and over, he slides so far down in the bed that we have to help pull him back to the top. Grover is always close by above, along with Sarah's new gift of a toy giraffe that whinnies.

Sarah and Martin have always shared secrets. When he was ten, she broke her promise of silence, adamant that I never tell she told. Martin had asked me to take him for an x-ray of his finger. He said he'd hurt it playing basketball. Thinking it was only a sprain, I said it didn't make sense to go to the emergency room. Sarah whispered that he'd really jammed it in a fight. I took him to the emergency room. The x-ray showed his finger was broken and needed a splint.

Now Sarah tells me that Martin confided in her that he can't believe he forgot to do "what every mother teaches her child to do— look both ways before you cross." He can't remember anything of the hours before the accident, but he knows he must have forgotten to look. I sense, from the way Sarah tells me what he told her, that he feels like a little boy again, ashamed that he let his mother down.

I think, *Who has not had a moment's inattention, and a stroke of luck that saves him from disaster? Mistakes keep happening, and sometimes luck runs out.*

CLINT SAYS WE can stay with him until Martin can go home, for months if we need to. But we want to live closer to Martin. The first four nights that he is in New England Rehab, we stay in nearby motels. The second night, after we've turned off our lights and Tom is asleep, a fire alarm sounds. I call the front desk. The clerk hangs up on me three times. The fourth time he says, "Stay in your room. It's a prank. People who go into the hallway may be robbed."

From our window I watch a fire engine wander through the parking lot, probably looking for smoke or flames they never find. Tom does not wake. It is a surreal passage in an interval when only the time with Martin seems real.

Looking for a place to live close to the hospital, I call Harvard classmates who live nearby. One man says he will look around for us.

The next day he and his wife send a shiny *Get Well* balloon that floats in Martin's room for weeks. Their card says:

> We were very sorry to hear about your accident. Lots of people that you have never heard of will be praying for you and your family.

I call real estate companies and tell their agents that we are looking for a place to rent. Only one has anything that could be rented for only a few months—a house whose owner is spending the winter in Florida.

We move into the little brown house in Woburn on Saturday, Martin's fifth day at New England Rehab. The house has a sunroom and, on the second floor, three bedrooms and the bathroom. The washer and dryer are in the basement. Sarah will have her own room when she is with us, and there is a bedroom for her friend, Emily, who may come from Santa Fe. It will be a cozy place for Christmas. We can stay until spring.

I imagine what I will do as our lives settle down—books I will read, and walks I will take with a college friend who lives nearby. Wendy and I had visited at the reunion before Martin was hurt, and the first week after his accident she loaned us a car. She invites us to join her family for Thanksgiving.

I READ MARTIN letters that have been sent to him and relay telephone messages from college friends who want to visit. We tell him he can decide whom he wants to see, and when. He does not reply, and we do not push. I think he is afraid. He tires fast, and he looks strange with one side of his head recently shaved and his plainly visible scars. He must wonder, *How okay am I?*

At Mass General, the nurses had us tell him over and over what had happened to him and where he was: "You were hit by a car. They brought you by ambulance to Massachusetts General Hospital. You are doing very well." At New England Rehab, they post a sign on the wall: *THIS IS NEW ENGLAND REHABILITATION HOSPITAL. TODAY IS FRIDAY NOVEMBER 5.* Everyone is determined to bring Martin back to us, here and now.

When the therapists are working with Martin, we make calls back to Santa Fe. We check in with my mother, keep track of messages, and do research to find the best doctors and therapists to work with Martin after we bring him home. While Martin, worn out after therapies and conversation, rests, I write thank you notes to people who have written or sent gifts.

ON SATURDAY, TOM'S mother and his older brother, Bill, visit New England Rehab. Tom had waited almost a week after Martin's accident before he called Bill. We did not want him to come until we were ready for his visit.

The last time we stayed with Bill and Grandma Maggie in their house in Arlington, just northwest of Cambridge, was a year ago, in the fall. Tom and Bill argued over and over. Tom wanted Bill to get cable television so Maggie could watch nature shows. He wanted Bill to fix his broken car so he could take Maggie out on drives. And he wanted Bill to turn on more lights in the house so Maggie would not have to sit in the dark.

Any façade of civility disappeared the day before we had planned to leave. That morning, Tom found his mother sitting in a corner of the kitchen, in the dark. He turned on the lights. Bill told Tom, "Stop acting as if you own this house."

Tom countered that their mother owned the house, not Bill, that the money Bill was saving was not anyone's but Maggie's, and that there was plenty of money to do little things to make her happy.

Bill declared that *he* paid the electric bill, and he could damn well decide what lights were turned on.

Tom said Bill was keeping their mother a prisoner and that *he* would pay the damn electric bill so Maggie didn't have to sit in the dark.

The argument traveled, erratically as quarrels do, and I left the room. I climbed to the third floor where we had been sleeping, packed my suitcase, and stripped our beds. Because Bill did not trust a repairman to come to the house when he was not there, the broken washing machine had never been fixed. Bill and his girlfriend washed laundry in the bathtub. I took our sheets and towels to the laundromat two blocks away.

When I came back with the clean dry sheets, Tom had packed his suitcase. We drove west across Massachusetts, to the friends we had planned to visit later that week.

Tom's and Bill's disputes stood for deeper issues. Tom hated being powerless to make his mother's life better. To me, Tom is the grownup in the family, the only brother who has married, the only one who is a father, the only one who has dogs and cats, the only one who owns a house, the only one who gardens. It amazes me that Bill and Henry still treat Tom as the baby brother.

"You're the grownup now," I tell Tom.

I am reluctantly learning how Tom's family dynamics are frozen in the Fifties. Henry, the middle brother, finds it easier not to become tangled in any disputes and keeps his distance. Perhaps still miffed by something long past, he sometimes calls Tom "Junior." He visits his mother at Thanksgiving and Christmas, and for occasional other brief stopovers. Bill, the oldest, keeps control. Tom, the youngest, fights the hierarchy. He doesn't win.

MY PARENTS HOPED for another child. The summer I was eight, I stayed with my Granny in England for several weeks while they traveled. When they came back, they said they had met a German boy in an orphanage and were thinking of adopting him. Although the adoption never happened, the phantom brother I might have had sometimes appears to me.

Years ago, I had a dream: my brother was a tall, dark-haired piano player at Harvard. I saw him in a coffee shop on Mount Auburn Street; and I adored him. Now, Martin, my tall, dark-haired musician son, lives in Lowell House on Mount Auburn Street.

I romanticized families with two or more children, even though my parents' own families were hardly ideal. My mother's wonderful brother died before I was born, and she called her other, living brother *cold* and *impersonal*. Her sister, she called *difficult*.

My father's unlikely brother never acknowledged his Jewish heritage. He changed his name. At the age of 42, a lean lieutenant colonel in the American Army, he died of a heart attack while playing tennis after supper.

Still, perhaps because no real brother or sister arrived to dispel my dreams, I still imagine families where brothers and sisters are best friends, and where children enjoy their aunts and uncles. Sarah and Martin make me happy. Tom's brothers are a disappointment, but I think I expect too much.

TWO AND A half weeks after Martin's accident, Tom invites Bill to visit Martin in New England Rehab. Bill brings Grandma Maggie with him. Maggie doesn't understand what has happened. Living completely in the present, she has no expectations of what ought to be, and seems untroubled by seeing Martin in his white netted bed.

Bill turns the conversation to when *he* was in the hospital more than twenty years ago. Tom is angry at Bill's inability to relate to Martin or to sympathize with what we have all gone through. I am simply relieved that he hasn't visited until now.

The next day, Clint comes, wearing a red jacket. Not wanting to overstimulate Martin, Tom and I wait in the hall while they talk. Clint has told us what he kept secret for weeks, that, before we got to Boston, he had claimed to be Martin's godfather and had gone into the Neurological ICU. Professionally knowledgeable about medical trauma, he didn't want us to ask him what he thought.

A week later, Martin does not recall either of those two visits, but he says he vaguely remembers Clint's red jacket. He has forgotten the dinners we had with Dave and Rachel before the accident, and he has no memory of the accident, no memory of Mass General, and no memory of his early days at New England Rehab.

He asks to hear the story of his lost days. It is as if he is listening to a tale about someone else. The telling does not awaken his memory. He has forgotten those harrowing weeks. His memory begins with Clint's red jacket.

> The most common cognitive impairment among severely head-injured patients is memory loss, characterized by some loss of specific memories and the partial inability to form or store new ones. Some of these patients may experience *post-traumatic amnesia* (*PTA*), either anterograde or retrograde. Anterograde PTA is impaired memory of events that happened after the TBI, while retrograde PTA is impaired memory of events that happened before the TBI. ["Hope Through Research," National Institute of Neurological Disorders and Stroke.]

WHEN MARTIN WAS four and Sarah almost seven, we went to see my father in his nursing home. Daddy, for safety, was tied into his chair by a cloth harness wrapped around his chest. It kept him from getting up and falling. He no longer spoke.

Sarah held back, aware of how different her grandfather was from her memory of him, and frightened of a grownup who did not act like a grownup. But Martin climbed onto Daddy's lap. He put his arms around his grandfather. I could feel my father's calmness, the closest he could come to happiness.

TOM REMARKS THAT self-consciousness involves both self-awareness and awareness of social norms. That Martin is self-conscious now is good. With regular clothing, he does not become uncovered as sometimes happened with a hospital gown. The people at the Woburn hospital say it is best for him to dress as he always has, and not to wear diapers. They are happy to change his clothes and the sheets if he has an accident. Martin stops swearing and is now polite with the nurses and aides.

> Most TBI patients have emotional or behavioral problems that fit under the broad category of psychiatric health. Family members of TBI patients often find that personality changes and behavioral problems are the most difficult disabilities to handle. Psychiatric problems that may surface include depression, apathy, anxiety, irritability, anger, paranoia, confusion, frustration, agitation, insomnia or other sleep problems, and mood swings. Problem behaviors may include aggression and violence, impulsivity, dis-inhibition, acting out, noncompliance, social inappropriateness, emotional outbursts, childish behavior, impaired self-control, impaired self-awareness, inability to take responsibility or accept criticism, egocentrism, inappropriate sexual activity, and alcohol or drug abuse/addiction. ["Hope Through Research," National Institute of Neurological Disorders and Stroke.]

Although some brain-injured patients never regain the social training they have lost, Martin retrieves both his self-awareness and his manners.

ONE DAY HE says to Tom and me, "I was in absolutely top physical and mental shape when this happened, and I will do whatever it takes to get back to where I was." He says the same thing to Dr. Suduikis.

Sue, the physical therapist, starts working with Martin the

morning after he arrives. He cries when she sets him in the wheelchair. He begs to lie down. After lying on his back or side for more than two weeks, his head throbs when he sits upright.

Right away, Sue tells Martin that her goal is to have him sit in the wheelchair for five minutes, one week hence. She makes clear that she is in charge and that Martin will do what she says. Tom and I cannot imagine that he can reach Sue's goal. For him, being upright—even for thirty seconds—is excruciating. I wonder whether each extra unnecessary day he stayed in Mass General set Martin back. I understand why people say that being in the hospital makes you ill.

Two days later, I write:

Martin walked today. I came back from lunch in the cafeteria and his room was empty. I found him in a chair in the Vermont Room, a place with chairs around a table, and a television. He was with his physical therapist Sue, the P.T. aide Betsy, and Tom. The wheelchair was in the hallway, ready to follow him so he could rest when he tired of walking. I wheeled it behind the procession as they walked toward the nurses' station.

Later I write,

Do you remember the first time we went outside (in the wheelchair)? We went out the door to the patio with the basketball hoop and the low wall. It was getting dark. The air was cool and fresh and we saw the oak tree you looked at from your window. Later—maybe another night—Kelly joined us. She was the skinny local girl who'd just graduated from Woburn High. She had me sign the papers when you arrived. She saw you were her age and she cried when she saw you could walk.

I do not cry when we see Martin walk, but my joy is greater than when he took his first steps more than nineteen years ago. Then, I knew that he would be walking sometime soon. Now I have not known, have not even asked, whether he will walk or read or dance or sing, and every step is a step into uncharted territory.

MARTIN HAS PHYSICAL therapy twice each weekday and once on Saturday—eleven sessions each week. Soon after his first steps, he becomes impatient at having to spend time with his physical therapist. He wants instead to talk with his physiatrist and to persuade her to increase the amount of liquid he is permitted to drink. We are still measuring every ounce, checking the notice board above his bed to see how many milliliters he is allowed each day.

Martin tells his physical therapist that he does not want to practice walking because he needs to discuss his doctor's ridiculous liquid limitation. Sue says, "Okay, then, let's go find Dr. Suduikis so you can ask her your questions." Motivated, he starts walking. He finds the doctor at the nurses' station, tells her he wants to discuss an important matter, and walks with her back to his room. He questions Dr. Suduikis a while. She agrees to raise his liquids limit, but not to eliminate it entirely.

A few days later, he is practicing hopping on one foot around the bright atrium at the center of the hospital. One more day, and he jogs indoors around the atrium. Martin is getting back to where he was, just as he said he would. By the time he leaves New England Rehab, Sue comes back winded from her outdoor jogs with him.

Martin also has eleven weekly sessions of speech therapy. Because his speech is fine—even in Spanish, as Maria, who mopped his floor at Mass General, confirmed—Cindy focuses on his attention span, his memory, and his thinking skills. She says her task is to prepare him for returning to college.

Tom and I leave whenever Cindy arrives. The papers with the words he struggles to write for her will later remind us of how he could hardly hold a pencil when he started speech therapy. His writing is large and uneven, sloping steeply down the page, bunched together where he runs out of space.

One day Martin complains to Cindy that a video she played for him was boring. She says, "Well of course your classes at Harvard aren't all interesting either."

"Yes they are," he tells her.

Cindy says her goal is to stretch the time he is able to focus on a task, but the worksheets she gives him to fill in remind us of the third-grade assignments he always hated. It is hard for him to pay attention to something that, long before his accident, would have bored him.

He says he is trying to be kind to Cindy, but working with her tires him. We arrange for the professor whose Einstein course Martin was taking before the accident to tape a lecture. Martin will watch it and try to take notes. At the start of the tape, Professor Galison dedicates his lecture to Martin. I picture the cathedral-like hall, its pews filled with students. I imagine each one, as Galison announces the dedication, thinking of Martin. It seems to me that the compassionate energy of so many students must be a powerful force for Martin's recovery.

Daily Living:
New England Rehabilitation Hospital, Part 2

Even the Idea demands
the work of hands,
the shape to feel.

Archibald MacLeish, *"The Ship in the Tomb"*

ELEVEN TIMES A WEEK, Martin has occupational therapy, to help him relearn what therapists call *activities of daily living*. His OTs are two young women—Cynthia, who is an intern, and her supervisor. One morning they announce they will help him relearn shaving.

"My dad helped me shave right after breakfast," Martin says.

Tom helped Martin assemble his washcloth and towel, face soap, shaving cream, and razor. He helped him keep track of the many steps—washing his face, leaving it wet, shaking the can of shaving cream, spreading the shaving cream on his face, shaving, rinsing the razor, rinsing his face, and drying his face.

Later, Tom says, "I was afraid that Martin would not be able to control his fine motor skills and would have trouble manipulating a very sharp object over his face. But I learned that shaving is like tying your shoelaces. It is a program that is routine enough that my fears were happily unnecessary."

MY FATHER LOVED rituals. He loved shaving. He lathered up his wooden bowl of Yardley shaving soap with a beaver-hair brush. When I needed the toilet, he happily stepped out of the bathroom and strolled around the small upstairs hall in his pajama bottoms, lathering his face with the soft brush.

More than twenty years ago, after the second operation to relieve pressure in his brain, he lay without speaking, hardly moving, for almost a week. Finally he spoke, asking what his chances were for survival. Soon after that, he asked for a razor. I set his razor on the bedside tray and turned away to pick up a hand mirror. When I looked back, Daddy was running the razor over his stubbly face.

"Hold on," I said, "I'll get water and shaving cream, and I'll hold the mirror."

"I'm just about done," he said, running his fingers over his smooth cheeks.

Martin was less gifted at shaving than my father, but then so is Tom, who can't shave without a mirror. But they did not need the OTs to teach Martin how to shave.

UNTIL YOU START from scratch, as most people only ever do with very young children, you do not think about how complex the *activities of daily living* are. Many brain trauma survivors never master them.

Several times the therapists offer to help Martin shower, but by the time they arrive after breakfast, Tom or I have already helped him. To get ready for his shower, he must take towels, shampoo, and soap to the shower room down the hall. He must take off his pants, underwear, shirt, slippers, and socks; put everything where it will stay dry; set the soap and shampoo in the shower stall; and place a towel on the floor to step onto when he gets out. In the shower, he has to keep one hand on the safety bar when he turns to wet his back, his front, his left side, his right side, and his hair. He has to wash each part and then rinse. Finally, he must step out; not drip on his clothes; dry himself; dress; and gather up towels, shampoo, and soap. Each time he showers, Martin needs less coaching and less help.

Many of the other patients are older, people who have had surgery to remove tumors or who are recovering from strokes. Martin is the youngest patient on the neurological wing. We tease him about his manly charms and suggest the young women OTs keep arriving earlier because they want to get there before he showers, hoping to help him.

We joke about how sad they look when once again they learn they have arrived too late. It gets so Martin delivers the punch line before we do.

One afternoon, he comes back late from jogging with Sue. Although he is tired, he asks, as he has done since he began leaving his room for therapies, "Has anyone come by while I was out?"

"Yes," I answer, "Dr. Keeler came by." Not many men are involved in Martin's care: Joseph Ratner, the psychiatrist; Alan, the nurse who suggested we get Martin regular clothes to wear; and Mark

Keeler, the neuro-psychologist who has interviewed Martin and given him several tests.

"What did Dr. Keeler want?" Martin asks.

"He was hoping to observe you taking a shower," I say.

For a moment Martin looks puzzled. Then he laughs. We are making jokes because we aren't so afraid anymore. His understanding them shows that his higher mental functions are intact. He has heard his parents laugh when he peed for the sake of all the Portuguese people and also for the sake of all the people of Brazil; he has made jokes ("I could tell you, but then I'd have to kill you"); and now he is laughing at silly innuendos. When we reflect on the subtlety of humor, on how much it depends on cultural understandings, and on why jokes are so hard to explain, we know that Martin's laughter signifies a great deal.

EACH MORNING WE drive clockwise around the east and south sides of Horn Pond, the Woburn town lake, to the hospital. At night we drive clockwise around the lake's west and north sides back to our cozy brown house.

On Martin's second Saturday in Woburn we arrange to bring him to the house, hardly believing that the doctors are letting him leave the hospital's safe cocoon.

Everything seems to happen in slow motion—walking to the car, helping Martin get in without bumping his head, driving the mile to our little house.

Although he needs to pee often, Martin says "no" when we offer a bucket so he won't have to go upstairs to use the bathroom. Each time he climbs the shiny wood stairs in his socks, I walk up below him.

When he comes down to the living room, I walk down backward, below him, ready to catch him if he falls. He moves slowly and does not slip.

We take him for a walk on the uneven grass beside Horn Pond. Ducks and geese waddle out of our way. When he needs to pee, Tom and Sarah and I find a bush and stand side by side to screen him. Back at the house, I cook fajitas, a Santa Fe favorite, with canned green chile no self-respecting New Mexican would use. We talk about missing the freshly roasted green chile we eat at home. While Tom and Sarah watch football in the sunroom. Martin naps, his head in Sarah's lap. We are a brief island of family.

Astonished by how far we have come and how fast, we also see how weak and vulnerable Martin is. He can go on a walk, but he needs us close by in case he stumbles. We help him where the ground is rough, and he never falls. We walk a short way slowly, and afterwards he needs to rest. Still, in less than two weeks, he has gone from crying in pain when Sue set him upright in a wheelchair to walking outdoors and climbing stairs. He entered the hospital strapped to a gurney, and now he walks outside in his own shoes.

Martin is much as he was before—funny, kind, alert to irony, empathetic. A Mass General social worker, whose duty was to prepare us for living with a brain-injured son, gave me pamphlets filled with terrible tales. In them, wives and parents told stories of TBI patients who lost their moral compass, became passive, or no longer expressed emotion. I skimmed a few pages and set the pamphlets aside. For Martin to lose physical abilities would be hard; to lose mental faculties worse; but to lose his spirit—I refuse to imagine that.

ONE DAY WHEN Martin is working with a therapist, I find Tom on the far side of the neurological wing. He is sitting with a man about our age. Ron is free to wander the wing, but not to leave. His ankle bracelet triggers an alarm if he steps into the elevator or opens the door to the stairs.

Ron isn't sure what happened to him. He thinks he fell off his mountain bike going down a hill, but he doesn't remember the hill or the fall. His nephew is the only person who has visited him. He has no other family.

Tom often sits with him when Martin is having therapy. Every day Ron asks how our son is progressing. He is careful not to intrude when we are in Martin's room, but one day he comes in to tell us that he had just heard Neil Young singing *Heart of Gold* on his Walkman. "The song made me think of you," he says.

On the day he leaves the hospital, he brings us a cassette of Neil Young's *Heart of Gold*. He has printed a note for us on notepaper shaped like an owl:

MARTIN

TOM + ELISE

A GIFT CASSETTE

FOR TRUE SOULS

WITH HEARTS OF <u>GOLD</u>

FROM

RON

We wish Ron had someone waiting for him at home, someone with a heart of gold.

RON IS THE one patient we ever talk with. A Thai woman in the room next door plays wailing music that wakes Martin every morning. We watch for her strikingly beautiful daughter in her short shorts and five-inch heels, but never speak with the woman or the daughter.

When Martin and I go to the shower room or when I get extra food for him from the staff room, I pass other patients. They sit propped in their chairs in front of the central nurses' and doctors' station.

At meal times the aides feed them. One man has a huge swollen head. Many of the patients look vacant and confused, damaged by catastrophes in their brains. We never see those who are better off. Able to feed themselves, they stay in their rooms even at meal times.

One patient who sits in a wheelchair near the doctors' station looks almost normal. Only a few years older than Martin, he wears molded plastic breast- and back-plates fitted to his body. He looks unbearably sad. A nurse confides, "He tried to die by jumping." I wonder, *When his body heals, will he try again?*

On the New England Rehab neurological wing, patients are expected to get better, but few will ever get well. We are grateful that Martin does not have a roommate, and that his room, closest to the atrium, is farthest from the nurses' and doctors' station. Days go by without our seeing any other patients.

Every afternoon Tom goes downstairs to talk with Danny, the young man who was once a patient here and who now sits behind the front desk in his wheelchair. We never learn what happened to him or what he was like before it happened, but we are sad for Danny because Martin has already passed him by in so many ways.

Martin worries out loud about how much school he is missing. Thinking he has more than enough reality to deal with, we don't say that he won't be able to go back to college for a good while. But after a week at New England Rehab, he remembers the year and the month. He knows how long he was in Mass General and how long he has been in New England Rehab. He says, "I guess I won't be finishing the semester."

ONE EVENING BEFORE supper, Martin is napping. I turn the television on low, hoping to catch the national news. A local news preview flashes on the screen—images of a wooden building in flames.

Martin opens his eyes. He moans and cries. I click the television off, but he has already gone to a painful place. It is as if his accident has just happened. He cannot glance at pain, even on a newscast, without suffering himself. I am stricken to have let this monster into his safe place. I do not turn on the television again.

BEING AN EMERGENCY medical technician helps Martin cope with what has happened, providing one realm where he feels competent. As soon as the ventilator came out and he could talk, he told his nurses at Mass General he was an EMT. At New England Rehab he asks, "What's my BP?" and then announces what his blood pressure was the last time they took it. He tells his psychiatrist that the only thing that makes him anxious is taking the anti-anxiety medications. He asks the psychiatrist to wean him off his medications, and Dr. Ratner creates a schedule reducing his dosages.

Once, Martin catches a nurse in an error, offering him a ten milligram tranquilizer dose instead of the five milligrams he is down to. He writes questions about his medications and liquid restrictions on a yellow pad.

Dr. Suduikis comes to his room and goes over the questions with him. His training as an emergency medical technician gives him the tools to understand his medical condition. It is important for him to regain some control, after having been so helpless.

By the time he leaves New England Rehab, he has worked with his doctors to discontinue all his medications and is taking only one daily multiple vitamin pill.

From my notebook:

> I keep hearing Sarah's voice as we walked to Central Square—"Everything has changed, Mom." I see Tom sitting on Sarah's sofa holding her phone, so still, asking questions. Gravity filled the room. In those few minutes, everything changed. I wanted only one thing, and there was no bargaining possible. Martin has so much to give the world.
>
> Today he asked his doctor, "How are you doing?" She was astonished, then said, "All right," and added it was an intense day. Is Martin the best listener they have ever had as a patient? He sees them, not just himself. Can we guess what he will make of this experience?
>
> Martin, these notes are for you, for the day when you want to look back and see us going through this time beside you.

The physical is so essential. When your systems fail, when you cannot control your body, you feel powerless, humiliated, beaten. We are vigilant to help you eat, use the bathroom, brush your teeth, because these things help to preserve your self-respect . . .

You are thirsty all the time, speak of water, of cranberry juice and soda, the nectar of the gods. Water; and fluid-restricted, you, desert son, cannot fathom how water can be bad. Your dry lips make me wonder. Are you right?

Flora [a nursing aide] saw your rash and ordered unbleached linens for your bed. Hope [another aide], from South Africa, saw you chafing at your ankle I.D. and asked the admitting office for a new one she could put on the other ankle, looser. Dr. Suduikis heard you say your head still hurt and changed your medication.

"How long will this go on?" you asked Hope. Patting your knee, she answered, "God can take care of things in the twinkle of an eye, but man does not know what will happen." There was radiance in her words. Dr. Ratner [the psychiatrist] said, "Martin will set his own pace." [The speech therapist] told you this morning, "It will take time." I could tell that she had told you that before. You said it back to her as if it were a lesson you are working to learn.

Like Martin, we are learning not to ask how soon or how long. We remember the clock setter in Mass General who said that his body told him all he needed to know. Many get well cards wish Martin a speedy recovery. We read them gratefully but, to us, speed is irrelevant.

Early Morning:
New England Rehabilitation Hospital, Part 3

Success is not final, failure is not fatal;
it is the courage to continue that counts.

Winston Churchill

MARTIN'S RECOVERY STARTS happening fast. Only two days after Sue said that in a week she'd have him sitting upright in the wheelchair for five minutes, he walks. The six to eight weeks Dr. Suduikis forecast for his rehab stay will be pulled back to twenty-two days. Therapists, doctors, and Tom and I all scramble to keep up.

Eight days after he came to New England Rehab, I write:

> *It's raining today. The leaves are still on the trees. We took you downstairs in your wheelchair on the weekend, and then outside to see the oak tree you look at from your window and to look up at your window.*
>
> *Yesterday you had four and a half hours of therapies. You wrote [dictated to me] a letter to Deborah Foster [your*

faculty advisor]. You looked at some of the cards that had
been arriving for you and us.

When you woke, after therapy and before supper, you
could not unravel your dreams from your waking state. You
made a terrible sound of sadness. . . . I fed you grapes and
tried to help you disentangle.

Martin's brain is working hard and is still vulnerable. He replenishes his energy with snacks between meals, finishing extra portions of applesauce saved from his meal tray and eating from the fruit basket Sarah's colleagues sent. Exhausted, he often naps after his therapies. I stay in his room then, writing to the many people who have called and written. I am grateful for this impulse to manners, taught me by my mother.

From my notebook:

You asked me to stop writing thank you notes and you
told me how sorry you were that you had caused me to suffer,
as you know I must have—not that you held yourself to
blame. And then you thanked me for being here with you.

MARTIN GROWS STRONGER, and sometimes he free associates out loud. One evening I record everything he says:

Toots and the Maytals have a song called "Peace."
[Martin sings the chorus.] Kris [his freshman roommate]—
what a beautiful guy he is. Even Tom Bok [the captain of the
Ultimate Frisbee team last year] was in my thoughts. Casey

[this year's Ultimate team captain] is just a really positive person, someone you can count on. I would like to make a tape of "Peace" for Sarah and the others.

If I hadn't gotten injured I might have gotten to see Peter. . . [a Santa Fe friend now studying engineering at Rice University who had planned to visit Martin in Cambridge]. Mr. Engineering.

All these women therapists ask me about my courses— more than fairly good. "Spoken Spanish through Theater" is really great.

He offers to recite the speech he memorized from a seventeenth-century play, *El Burlador de Sevilla*, the speech of a heartless seducer. Lying in bed, he recites the long speech in Spanish. He finishes, and declares, "I don't sympathize with the character at all. I respect women."

Martin is so emotionally open that, just as he had to struggle to separate his dreams from reality, he needs to safeguard the difference between the coldhearted character's attitudes and his own feelings.

THREE YOUNG MEN, Sarah's friends from Santa Fe, are the first visitors close to Martin in age. They arrive with a huge yellow sunflower.

I watch Martin with them—how he sits up in his bed, how he speaks, and how he watches himself being watched. He is both aware of himself and relaxed. The friends, whom we have known for years, are more at ease than I imagined they could be. Childhood pals, they are traveling together after college. Only later do I remember what they have gone through before coming here. Barely two months ago, Swissair flight 111 crashed into the Atlantic Ocean. Aaron's father died along with 228 others. Marked by tragedy, they are eager to offer comfort.

ON SUNDAY, NOVEMBER 15, I drive Tom to Providence. He will fly home to New Mexico tomorrow, patch our leaking roof, gather our winter clothes, and come back to Woburn in a week.

At last, Martin responds when I remind him that his college friends want to visit. Perhaps reassured by how he felt with the friends from Santa Fe, he says three of his Harvard friends can come by after supper.

When I return from driving Tom to Providence, Dave, Justin, and Rachel are waiting in the hospital atrium. I lead them to Martin's room and show them where they can sit—chairs, Martin's bed, the empty bed, even the wheelchair. Two of them take regular chairs, and one stands. No one takes the wheelchair. Is it too intimate a reminder of Martin's terrible injury and of the hopeless hours they waited outside Mass General's emergency room?

Aching for a hot bath and bed, I leave Martin with his friends. The next morning he sleeps late. I wake him so he can have breakfast before his first therapist arrives. He had been awake and with his friends until ten, long past his usual bedtime.

AN EXOTICALLY STRIKING doctor comes in after supper another evening. Nadia Kassissieh is an electro-diagnostician, a dark-eyed woman in her early forties. She takes us three floors down in the elevator. Martin says that the hospital's basement swimming pool must be nearby. He smells chlorine in the air.

We follow Dr. Kassissieh into a dim room full of boxes and machines on counters, on chairs, and on the floor. She carries one large box with wires coming out of it over to a table. Martin sits beside it. He takes off his shirt. I squeeze into a corner.

Dr. Kassissieh uses electric stimuli to study muscle tissue. Her immediate goal is to find out whether the nerves in Martin's arm below his fractured left scapula, or shoulder blade, are functioning properly. She hooks an electrode to his hand and slowly pushes a needle into his biceps. On a machine that looks like an early television screen, a white wave appears in the black. Its frequency and amplitude fluctuate. When the doctor moves the needle in his arm, the machine crackles. When she holds the needle still, the machine is silent.

He says the needle feels a little weird but doesn't hurt. The doctor tests his right biceps, then his left. She says that, although the wave on the screen doesn't tell her much, the crackling sounds do. "Can you hear the noise change?" she asks as she moves the needle. He can. I can't.

She thinks a nerve in his left shoulder is damaged, probably from the impact that broke his scapula in five places. She wants a CT scan to tell her more.

Martin says his left foot sometimes feels a bit numb. I remember something he does not know—in the ICU his left side was slower than his right in responding to pinches and commands. His left foot was slowest of all. We feared his left leg might be paralyzed. Now, as Dr. Kassissieh gently probes the muscles of his left leg with her needle, she says that he has tarsal tunnel syndrome, a pinching of a nerve that passes through the ankle to the foot. (Tarsal tunnel syndrome refers to the ankle as carpal tunnel syndrome refers to the wrist.)

She thinks the problem is mild and will improve with time.

When the session in the dark basement chamber is over and Martin is putting on his shirt, I look out into the corridor. His freshman roommate, Kris, puts his finger to his lips to hush me and backs around the corner. When Martin comes out, Kris greets him with a big hug. Upstairs, I leave them together and go home to our little brown house.

MARTIN NOTICES AN unevenness in his upper front teeth. He has never had a cavity, never had anything but teeth cleaning done in a dentist's office.

In nearby Winchester, a photo of the dentist's red-haired daughter hangs on his office wall. She is a Harvard student too, and the dentist knows about Martin. After he confirms that his front tooth is chipped, he bonds a coating behind the tooth to strengthen it. Then he files it smooth. When he finishes, he announces that he has filed Martin's eyeteeth a tiny bit too, to make his smile more beautiful.

I am speechless. He has done something irreversible, without Martin's knowledge or permission. I try to hide my anger, hoping Martin will receive the information with equanimity. Unlike me, he is slow to anger.

As we drive back to the hospital, he says the dentist should not have done anything to his perfectly good teeth. I agree. We both try not to show how hurt we feel. We cannot change what has been done, and I do not want to add to Martin's sense of injury by making a scene.

Our first foray for care away from New England Rehab has gone badly. We let the matter go.

Later, although I still resent the dentist's act, I realize he filed Martin's eyeteeth because he wanted to do something special for him. He had no idea how important it was, in the disaster we were weathering, for Martin and for me to control what was done. I am angry for a long time before I realize he only meant the best.

Leaving New England:
("You can't speed up time.")

And this, then,
is the vision of that Heaven of which
we have heard, where those who love
each other have forgiven each other,

where, for that, the leaves are green,
the light a music in the air,
and all is unentangled,
and all is undismayed.

Wendell Berry, "To My Mother"

ON NOVEMBER 6, I wrote in my notebook that I doubted Martin would be well enough to go to our friend Wendy's home for Thanksgiving. Eleven days later, his case manager tells me that New England Rehab will release him the day before Thanksgiving.

The case manager has hinted that Martin's rehabilitation might be shorter than the originally projected six to eight weeks, but she had to wait for final word from the weekly meeting of nurses, therapists, and doctors. Now they all agree that after one more week in the hospital, Martin can go home. Tom does not need to fly back from New Mexico with our winter clothes. We will fly to him.

In the week and a half since we moved to Woburn, I have read nothing and have gone on no walks with friends. One bright morning, Tom went to the hospital early and I walked from our house to the lake. I found an overgrown path and climbed up the hill to the hospital. Aside from that, my days have been too full for anything but Martin, obligations, and sleep. My life has not settled down as I imagined it would when we moved to our little brown house.

The idea of traveling with Martin frightens me. His needs— for food, sleep, and bathroom—all have to be taken care of right away. Will I be able to manage everything? When Sarah offers to fly home with us, I realize that, if she comes to Boston to help us get ready to leave, the airline staff can help us change planes in Minneapolis, and Tom will meet us in Albuquerque.

Sarah comes to Boston on Friday afternoon. She is taking the next week off work to be with Martin and me.

We sleep together in the double bed. The last time we shared a bed, it was her futon in New York. The call about Martin's accident woke us.

In the morning, I tiptoe to the bathroom. I put in my contact lenses. My vision is fuzzy. Has my anxiety affected even my sight? Then I see a lens case on the ledge by the mirror. It is my lens case. I have put Sarah's lenses in my eyes. My vision is fine.

When I come back to the bedroom, my daughter, who always wants to sleep as long as possible, is getting dressed. She had planned to sleep late, and later in the day to walk along the lake and up the hill to the hospital, but we drive there together. She has chosen her mother and her brother over her need for sleep.

On Saturday, Martin wants to go out to dinner. I protect his head with my hand as Sarah helps him into the car, the way you see cops guiding people in handcuffs into police cars. We have to get on the highway to find a restaurant. One summer in college, Tom drove a cab in Boston, and he usually drives us when we're around here. Now I hate our under-powered rental car, hate the Saturday night traffic, hate the right lanes that turn into exit lanes, and hate how each car moves up too close to the one ahead of it.

One restaurant offers us a table in an hour. When the hostess at the next place says twenty minutes, we decide to wait on a bench in the entry. Dozens of people crowd the waiting area, talking and laughing. The outside door opens and closes constantly. Bombarded by noise and activity, Martin looks worried and weak. He is too hungry for us to consider leaving. I get him a juice drink to raise his blood sugar. I ask for a basket of bread. I wonder how the hostess cannot see that we need special care, and why she makes us wait. Why doesn't she give us the next free table?

Except for that one disastrous meal, Sarah and I eat lunch and supper in the hospital cafeteria with Martin. Patients get a discount. When the cashier asks Martin if he is a patient, he asks me, "Why does he think I'm a patient?"

He wonders whether it is because of his hair, with the long hair on the left combed toward the shaved right side where his hair is starting to grow back. He asks if he looks funny in some other way.

I don't tell Martin how his head tips to one side, or how intense he looks as he chooses his food. I say, "It's probably your hair."

When Sarah and I take him to his dorm room at Harvard to choose what to take home, several friends join us there. Martin announces that he is going for a walk with Rachel. I want to tell her, *Help him with stairs*, and *Hold onto him all the time*, but I don't.

I walk a tightrope between protecting Martin and putting him in touch with what is really happening. It is like a speeded up replay of motherhood—moving from being my son's everything to launching him into the world on his own, from protecting him to setting him free. And it happens fast. Each day I need to do less and to let him do more alone. It is harder letting go now than the first time. This time I know how much can go wrong, and I know the pain of almost losing him.

EARLY ON, IN the ICU, the nurses told Martin that he had been hit by a car, that he had had brain surgery, that he was in Massachusetts General Hospital in Boston, and how many days he had been there. When he was still in the ICU, Martin said he wanted to call his advisor to let her know where he was. We told him she knew about the accident, that she had called us, and that the story was in the *Crimson*, the student newspaper. He asked to see the *Crimson*.

The morning after the accident, the *Crimson* ran a front page story with a photo, captioned *TRAGIC SCENE*, of the car that hit Martin, its fender dented and windshield shattered. I had not brought the paper with me, for fear he would want to see it. Every few days, he asked again.

After about a month, I think Martin is strong enough and bring him the paper. He reads and gives it back, saying nothing.

I need to face the emotional distress that remains from our

first reading of the *Crimson* at Mass General. The story said:

> *Witnesses said they saw [Martin] step into the street*
> *in front of the car just after 11 p.m. They said the car tried to*
> *stop but hit [Martin], who was a few feet from the curb.*

To us, the wording suggested that Martin had intentionally stepped in front of the car. For Tom and me, there was no reason to imagine this was true, but still, that first day in the hospital, nothing made sense and anything was possible.

We asked Martin's roommate what he remembered of that night. Dave recalled going with Martin to a study break. Afterwards, he said, Martin left their room. As he walked out, Martin ruffled Dave's hair and said he was going to visit Rachel. He seemed fine, playful. Nothing amiss.

Rachel never talked with us about that night, and we never learned whether she had been waiting for Martin. We know only that she had been among those waiting for word at Mass General that dark night.

When Tom and Clint went to where Martin was hit on Memorial Drive, it became clear that either the witnesses or the reporter had got the story wrong. No one could have seen him step off the curb *in front of the car*, because he was hit in the second lane from the curb, not *a few feet* but *many yards* away from the curb.

A week before Martin and I fly home, I go to the *Crimson* building. I ask to see the reporter who wrote the story. When he comes to meet me, I notice that he is younger than my son.

I ask him who the *witnesses* he interviewed were. He says all three were so shaken they would not give their names. I explain that

Martin was hit in the middle lane, not the curb lane. Therefore he could not have stepped *into the street in front of the car...a few feet from the curb.* I suggest that his witnesses were too shaken to know what they saw, and that the second and third may have only repeated what they heard the first witness say, which was itself inaccurate.

I tell the reporter he should have checked the witnesses' accounts against the evidence. I explain that his words added to our fear—that he made us wonder, until Tom and Clint examined the accident scene, if Martin had wanted to hurt himself.

The reporter does not respond. He does not acknowledge his carelessness.

WHEN DR. KEELER, the neuro-psychologist, tests Martin in preparation for his discharge, he is puzzled. Martin tests in the superior range in many areas, but there are anomalies. On one problem set, he does well on the easy tasks, poorly on the moderate ones, and well on the most challenging questions. To me this makes sense: easy is so easy he gets it right, moderate is too dull to bother thinking over, and hard is fun to figure out.

Martin's scores on a stimulus response test also perplex Dr. Keeler. When he asks him about that test, Martin says he tried pushing the response button with different fingers and also with his thumb, trying to figure out how to react fastest. The results, of course, are worthless. Was he afraid the test would show that he is not as well as he seems? Or was he just bored?

Dr. Keeler asks me if Martin is different from before his injuries. He mentions that he is often quiet for a long time, sometimes for more than a minute, before answering a question. I say that he has always been slow to respond, considering and formulating his answers before speaking. I cannot tell if he is slower now.

I so want to perceive Martin as fundamentally unchanged that I know I can't be objective. To help Dr. Keeler, I get Lowell House to give me an envelope, sealed, with his high school teachers' confidential college recommendations. His application essays must also be in the envelope. They, too, will help Keeler get a sense of Martin before the accident.

I remember his essay about rock climbing:

> I love the feel of rope, the clinking of carabiners, the smell of the rubber, leather, and sweat of my rock shoes. I have a passion for rock climbing. To be out there against the rock, gripping its solidness, wind blowing across my face; there's nothing like it.
>
> I climb on cliffs near Los Alamos, New Mexico, overlooking the valley of the Rio Grande. The view is awesome. Up the valley, to the north, the Sangre de Cristo Mountains stretch all the way to Colorado. In the south are the Sandia Mountains, rising 5,000 feet above Albuquerque. To the east: plains, mesas, and jagged valleys run like veins. Over a thousand feet below, the brown water of the Rio Grande snakes its way along the canyon floor.
>
> Each climb is like a challenge in life. I have to find strength and determination within myself. As climber Carlos Buhler put it, "To continue climbing in the face of enormous obstacles broadens our vision of what we can accomplish

anywhere." There are also challenges that cannot be overcome; not every rock is climbable.

For me, being out there climbing puts things in perspective. When you put your life in the hands of your climbing partner, other things seem less important. . . . I sometimes need to step back and look at life in a different way to maintain my wits. . . .

Rock climbing . . . requires not only power and skill, but confidence, stamina, concentration, perseverance, and conviction. . . .

To overcome . . . fear, I need to be relaxed and to have confidence. . . .

Martin at seventeen was a philosopher. At twenty, he is who he needs to be to meet the challenges he faces. He has power and skill, stamina, concentration, perseverance, and conviction. And he is stepping back and looking at life in a different way.

TWO DAYS BEFORE Thanksgiving, on his last Tuesday at New England Rehab, Martin prepares a breakfast. The meal serves as his graduation rite from occupational therapy. His therapist, Sarah and her friend Emily, who has come to visit, and I are his guests. To show mastery of an *activity of daily living,* he planned the menu and went shopping with Cynthia the day before. He serves orange juice he pours and French toast he cooks. He has set the table with everything we need: knives, forks, napkins, glasses, plates, butter, and syrup. His timing is perfect and the breakfast delicious.

At eleven, Martin and Sarah and I go to a final conference with Dr. Suduikis and all his therapists. Sarah's presence makes up for Tom being gone.

Sue began Martin's physical therapy before he could even sit up. Now she gets out of breath jogging with him. She wants him to keep working on speed, strength, and coordination. She reminds him to guard against fatigue, and to take breaks.

Cynthia, who has tried so hard to find OT tasks to challenge Martin, warns him that he did not scan carefully enough for cars when they walked to the supermarket to shop for the breakfast he made. She reminds him that fatigue makes it hard to pay attention to details like choosing safe paths. "Take enough time," she says.

The speech therapist advises him to avoid lengthy classes when he returns to college. Instead of seminars that meet once a week for several hours, he should take hour-long classes that meet several times each week. "Get extra time as you need it," she says.

She also notes that he has extended his attention span—only a minute or two long when she first worked with him—to forty minutes. Later that day, Martin points out to Sarah and me the irony of discussing with him his forty-minute attention span near the end of an hour-long meeting.

Dr. Suduikis wants Martin to find out if New Mexico has any legal requirements for driving after brain injury. She warns that he will react differently to alcohol or recreational drugs after his injury. She assures him that he has the intellectual capacity to return to Harvard. It is up to him, she says, but she thinks returning in January would be premature.

Suduikis says Martin has benefited from having Tom and

Sarah and me around. Partly because of us, the rehabilitation that was expected to last six to eight weeks has taken just three. She warns that the next stage will be difficult, not the steep mountain we have been climbing, but a long plateau, without the landmarks that have heartened us in our journey so far. She tells Martin that she expects he will continue improving for a year. She says, "You can't speed up time."

At the end of the conference, Martin thanks everyone in the room, one by one. I say that Dr. Suduikis, the therapists, and nurses all deserve credit for Martin's remarkable progress, that we noticed Dr. Suduikis coming into the hospital on many of her days off, and that she worked the whole week she was ill.

THAT LAST EVENING at New England Rehab, after supper, Martin asks us to drive him down the hill to the supermarket where he and Cynthia shopped for breakfast. He chooses azaleas, cyclamen, and chrysanthemums for his favorite nurse, for Dr. Suduikis, and for his three main therapists. Double checking with us because he is color blind, Martin has clear opinions about which flower and what color is right for each person. He gets single sunflowers for the men— his nurse Alan, his psychiatrist Joseph Ratner, and his neuro-psychologist Mark Keeler. He chooses more sunflowers for Flora, who ordered unbleached linens for his bed, for his case worker, and for the counselor he went to visit when he saw a rock climbing poster on her office wall.

Bombarded by the noise and fluorescent glare of the supermarket, Martin looks dazed. He moves as if in a dream. I suggest that Sarah or I finish checking out so the other one of us can drive him up the hill and he can get ready for bed. Martin says no; he wants to change the pink foil wrapping that clashes with the bronze chrysanthemum and the orange bow that spoils the red azalea. With the floral clerk's help, he changes all the plants' wrappings. He insists on going through the checkout line and on helping Sarah and me carry the plants and flowers up to his room.

Early the next morning, Sarah helps pack our suitcases with Tom's and my belongings. We clean the little brown house, leave the key in the mailbox, and go to New England Rehab.

Martin gives each person the flowers he chose last night.

The elevator doors are so slow, set to accommodate wheelchairs and unsteady patients, that I run up and down the stairs with Martin's things. I meet his psychiatrist on the landing. For the first time, Dr. Ratner is not reserved and formal. He says how much he likes Martin and how happy he is that he has made such amazing progress. His warmth surprises me and my heart beats faster as I run up the last flight of stairs.

Driving down the hill from the hospital feels like leaving home. We are elated to be leaving, and frightened to be on our own.

CLINT'S HOUSE, NEAR Harvard Square, is our first stopover on the journey home. Clint lives with assorted antiques from his founding father heritage and with mementos from his other heritage, the grandmother who lived on a ranch in Montana. The condo is several stories high, with an open space in its center. A wall of rough sawn boards runs from the living room's wood stove up to his office in the loft. Hanging on the boards is a poster of a desert landscape by a painter also named Clint Smith, who Clint teasingly claims to be, on the side, in his spare time, when he's not being a Boston lawyer. There's a fishing creel hanging on the wall, and a trophy head of a deer. Clint calls the trophy *Bambi* and says that, after Bambi, he never shot another deer.

Every evening Clint comes home from work late, pours himself a glass of vodka, and loosens his tie. He likes having us there, having us sleeping in his guest room and on his sofas, having Sarah and her friends in his house, bringing our unpredictability into his ordered life.

I walk behind Martin as he climbs in his socks up the slippery wooden stairs. While he naps, Sarah and Emily go to Mass General to pick up his medical records.

That evening, Sarah calls her boyfriend in Washington, D.C. Close to ten years older than she, he feels ready to settle down. She does not. She sits on Clint's stairs, agreeing to end their relationship. Afterward, she lets me hold her, but only for a minute. We both understand that, under other circumstances, we would focus more on her life. I want her to know that, despite my concentration on Martin's needs, she is enormously important to me.

I give her a sparkly evening bag, an early present for her December first birthday. I spotted it when I was buying a carry-on suitcase to hold Martin's x-rays, CT scans, MRIs, and medical records so I didn't have to risk them as checked luggage.

AT SIX-THIRTY the next morning, the Boston airport is almost empty. Right away, the ticket agent calls for a wheelchair for Martin, who looks pale and thin, and has odd hair. Sarah strokes

Martin's hands and forehead as the agent writes his ticket. When he rewrites my five-week-old ticket home from Providence, he doesn't add the change fee he's supposed to charge.

A porter pushes the wheelchair to the gate. He helps us onto the plane long before official boarding begins. He lets Sarah come into the cabin with us even though she is not a passenger. We have seats by the bulkhead so Martin can stretch out and sleep. The porter helps stow the heavy suitcase with the medical records. Sarah tucks Martin in with a pillow and two blankets. She will spend Thanksgiving with Emily, and, in less than a month, will fly home for Christmas.

In the Light

Beauty can spontaneously occur at any moment given the proper circumstances, context, or point of view. Beauty is thus an altered state of consciousness, an extraordinary moment of poetry and grace.

Leonard Koren,
Wabi-Sabi for Artists, Designers, Poets & Philosophers

OUR FAMILY WAS FORTUNATE in more than the good hospitals and helpful insurance companies we came across. Martin had a good mind, and he had disciplined it. He was physically strong and had great stamina from playing on the Ultimate Frisbee team.

Tom and I were able to leave our real estate business to care for him. Sarah's colleagues made it easy for her to be with us every weekend, for the week she helped me get ready to bring Martin home, and at Christmas.

Our Harvard connections opened doors. The Health Services director persuaded the Mass General doctors to talk with us, and our classmates' colleagues and friends, including Dr. Altman and Dr. Woo, went out of their way to help us.

Even Martin's own temperament was in his favor. Some of his early traits, stubbornness and recklessness, did not make him an easy child, but, in time, those qualities ripened into willpower and courage.

WHEN HE WAS six and seven, Martin sometimes became angry, packed his backpack, and ran away. He made sure we heard him bang the front door as he left. I would follow at a distance and find him sitting in the arroyo, the dry wash that crosses our land, his back against the sandy bank, facing away from home. I would sit in the arroyo, fifty or more feet away from him. After a while, I might say, "I'm hungry." A minute later, I'd ask, "Do you want supper?" I'd sit in the sand until he got up and walked back to the house, well ahead of me.

When he was younger still, Martin was a notably *noncompliant* child. For several months, a woman doing research on four-year-olds visited us once a week to "observe" him.

Lynn later showed us a graph she had made for her dissertation. She titled it *Degrees of Compliance*. Of the twenty children she studied, nineteen clustered close to its center or lay in the region to the right, approaching *extreme compliance*. The one child at the graph's far left, its *noncompliant* frontier, was our son.

Lynn had correlated each child's compliance with his or her galvanic skin response, respiration, and pulse, all of which she had measured in her office. Lynn hooked Martin up to various gauges, telling him he would hear tones through the earphones she put on him. She said he would react to what he heard with changes in perspiration, breathing, and heartbeat.

He asked, "Do I have to?"—meaning, *Do I have to react?* Then he proceeded to baffle Lynn. When the tones sounded in his ears, she could measure no change in his galvanic skin response, respiration, or pulse.

Sixteen years later, Martin baffled Dr. Keeler at New England Rehab with his puzzling responses to tones and lights. I imagine that, just as he chose to exercise great self-control during Lynn's experiments, tuning out the tones in his earphones, he did something similar with Mark Keeler's tests.

I may have learned more than Lynn did from her studying Martin. While he and I were being observed during that hour between supper and his bedtime, I began to watch myself. Because he could be so difficult, I realized that I was choosing not to let him see himself as difficult. I did not ask him to do anything he was likely to balk at unless it was non-negotiable—like putting away toys, getting in his night clothes, or brushing his teeth. Sometimes I conned him into helping, saying, "Could you help me—oh never mind, I'll ask Sarah or Tom. It's too hard for you." Then he would ask what I needed, and prove that he was up to the task. I think my hands-off tactics encouraged Martin to become self-reliant. He developed a temperament well suited to taking charge of his own recovery.

ALTHOUGH MARTIN WAS bright, his first-grade teacher noticed several areas where he seemed below average— including fine motor skills and coordination. A diagnostician recommended therapy, which would take him out of the classroom several times a week. Tom and I didn't like the idea. We agreed—not understanding why at the time—that his self-confidence was shaky. We wanted to spare him the stigma of being pulled out of the classroom.

It took years for us to recognize how his pre-school had colored his experience. We often brought him to school late, but the school's director never confronted Tom and me, the parents who didn't have their act together. Instead she frowned on our child. Women who taught with her told us, years later, that Martin was also one of several high energy boys who suffered from the director's disapproval. At the end of Martin's first year in public school, all we knew for sure was that he would not respond well to needing special help.

I asked the diagnostician to explain the treatments therapists would offer. To develop fine motor skills, they would give tasks requiring finger dexterity. "What if we ate a couple of meals with chopsticks every week?" I suggested. She liked the idea.

The therapist might hold Martin in a blanket and push him so he had to work to regain his balance. "Maybe Tom could do more rough housing, lying on the floor and grabbing Martin's ankles—would that work?" I asked. Another good idea.

In time, we thought up many ways to do therapy without Martin realizing what we were up to. I noticed that some things he did, which previously I might have cut short, were variations on the diagnostician's suggestions. She encouraged us to crawl around on the floor with him—and we did. He crawled around on his own too, something Sarah had not done at his age. Had his early eagerness to stand up cut short those important hours of crawling? I remember him pulling himself up, gripping my skirt to stay upright as I washed dishes, until his tired legs collapsed. Had his limited crawling kept him from developing a strong sense of balance, from improving his fine motor skills?

I taught myself to slow down when Martin stepped off the sidewalk and walked along the curb, thinking that he was instinctively working to correct a deficit. I became more patient with him, and I saw how often his quirky impulses led him to practice something helpful for his development.

In the mountains, Tom nailed a two-by-four board on edge between two stumps, and both our children spent hours "walking the plank," thereby improving their balance. I put together one-dish meals, leftover this and chopped that, meals that Tom and Sarah and Martin came to call "one of Mom's numbers." We ate my *numbers* with chopsticks.

Our early experiences with therapy may have prepared us for helping Martin through his recovery. We had discovered how easy it is to make therapy a part of our daily lives.

WHEN MARTIN WAS eight, he had trouble getting ready for school on time. (And when he was in high school, he was well-known for still tying his shoes when his friends came to pick him up.) When he missed the school bus, we drove him the two miles to school.

One evening, we told him we would help him get up earlier but that from now on, if he missed the bus, he would have to walk to school. Soon after, he missed the bus. After he had brushed his teeth, tied his shoes, and put his homework in his backpack, we reminded him he had to walk to school. Tom followed in the car, making sure Martin crossed streets safely and watching him take shortcuts across the hospital's fields and parking lots, all the way to school. There was no anger from

Martin or from us, and no tears. He never missed the bus again.

At his most difficult—and several of our friends agree that he seemed a remarkably difficult child—Martin was never a bully. A trickster, yes. When my mother took him to the Plaza for a treat, he hid from her in the center of J.C. Penney's circular clothing racks. He so frightened her that she never took him on an outing alone again. He fought with and teased his big sister. He could be incredibly contrary with Tom and me.

But when I was sick, Martin brought me food and glasses of juice. With younger children, he was gentle. Gradually, between the ages of eight and twelve, he became easy to live with. He stopped scaring me, or perhaps he learned to be a daredevil only when out of my sight. He and Tom went backpacking. He made friends who played elaborate spy games and biked mountain trails. At school, he and his friends directed and acted in avant garde plays.

Sarah says that Martin, as the second child, had an easier time than she, that she trampled down the brambles and he just strolled behind her on the path she'd trampled smooth. I answer her, "At least Tom and I didn't keep making the same mistakes."

By the time Martin came along, we had learned to quiet our parental expectations and to give him at least the illusion of considerable independence.

SARAH AND I often figure out what we think by articulating our thoughts, in writing or as we speak. Tom and Martin seem to think things out before they speak. Tom is usually in a hurry. Martin is patient. He considers carefully. He takes a long time to make up his mind.

When Martin makes a decision, he stays with it. While he was still in high school, he wanted to take the emergency medical technician course. Sarah and I both thought that would be a mistake. Because he preferred her advice to mine, I asked her to talk with him. One summer evening, I washed dishes and eavesdropped as she talked with him about the tough courses he was about to take in his senior year. She told him how much time college applications would take. She reminded him to save time for plays and for making music.

Martin decided to wait to become an EMT, but he did not abandon his plan. In the fall after he graduated from high school, he enrolled in the community college and became an EMT.

MARTIN'S SLOWNESS TO make decisions, and his holding fast to what he has chosen, helped him in his healing from his traumatic brain injury. He kept working at his physical coordination, strength, and stamina. He devised new therapies for himself, took up tap dancing, learned the flute, and practiced drawing. He didn't drown his troubles in alcohol or drugs, which would have hampered his recovery. I heard tragic stories of others who, confronted with similar challenges, did not persevere. They did not do well.

Knowing how much good fortune we have had, sometimes I question whether I should tell our story, whether it might be too painful for others less fortunate to hear. If Martin had even partial paralysis, or personality changes, or mental impairment, I don't know how we would have weathered those disappointments.

Our lives continue, and there will be challenges,

disappointments, and worse. I examine what we have been given so far, trying to learn its lessons, hoping to be ready for whatever is next.

Coming Home:
Thanksgiving 1998

. . . though I walk through the valley of the shadow of death . . .

Psalm 23

TOM IS AT THE ARRIVAL gate in Albuquerque. We thought he would be back with us in New England by now. Instead, we're coming home to him.

Back at last in Santa Fe, he tucks Martin into his bed for a nap. I drive to my mother's. Hugging her, I begin to sob. All my bravery is used up. Mother holds me for a minute. Then she says, "Don't cry."

How can I not cry? I ache, feeling I am no longer the daughter to be consoled. How I wish she would say what I say to my children—"Go ahead and cry." Not now, but years later, Mother tells me that my coming to her so soon after we came home moved her, as did my tears. Why can't she tell me now?

Another afternoon, I have tea with her. I look at the framed scroll commemorating her brother, Noel, on the wall. He "served King and Country in the world war of 1939-1945 and gave his life to save mankind from tyranny." Noel played the piano, and he left apple cores around the house the way Tom leaves his carrot ends. He could not become the doctor he longed to be because the family did not have money for medical school. My mother was twenty-six when he, a medic in France, drove over a land mine and died. Noel is my middle name, one way she keeps his memory alive.

Since the day Tom and I drove to Mass General, leaving our daughter in New York, I have imagined how Sarah would suffer if her brother died. Now I feel my mother's loss as I never have before.

We do not talk about these things. Mother has told me many everyday details of life in London during the war—about leaving water in the tub after her bath to be ready to douse small fires, and about the friends who lived in the three floors above her and who gathered in her ground floor flat on bad bombing nights. She told me about the night she left the Savoy to walk home and watched the beautiful churches burning in the Strand. But she does not talk about her brother's death. She does not go to that place of deep sorrow. Or perhaps she does, but does not take me there with her.

OUR HOUSE IN Santa Fe is easy to make ready for Martin. There is only one step from the living room up to the bedroom hallway. With doors open and night lights on, I sleep as lightly as when the children were little, listening for him to stir, ready to go help him if he wakes. We brace a chair against his bed in case he rolls to the edge.

From my notebook:

> *Lying here, in my bed, the same bed, in my nightie, the same nightie, ready to sleep, after reading, warm with my hot bottle, even the act of writing is so familiar and yet it is not at all the same. This morning before dawn I woke to tears and you, my good husband, tried to wake me from my dream. It's not a dream, I told you, it's nothing I will wake from. It's our poor baby, having to suffer so. I treasure my life because he needs me, because I can comfort him and help, time the jumping jacks he practices. . . . We're on the plateau, leveling out for a long push, committing to determination and patience.*

TOM HAS SCHEDULED medical appointments for Martin. We sense how fast he is recovering when he says that from now on he wants only one parent to accompany him to any appointment.

Our family doctor, stunned after reading the records I brought from Mass General and New England Rehab, holds Martin in a long hug. They talk in private for an hour.

After Martin and Tom go to the neurologist whom friends have recommended, Elizabeth Lakind, they tell me that she is the sharpest doctor they have met. She warned Martin not to get overly tired or hungry and to stay away from three things: Sudafed and MSG, both of which alter the brain's chemistry, and chiropractors. She told him, "You have done something no one your age should have to do— come face to face with your own mortality." Dr. Lakind has the wisdom and temperament that Jerome, our Jungian analyst friend, advised me to seek out for Martin a long month ago.

Martin's new physiatrist, who will set up and supervise his therapies, is many months pregnant. I am happy that the woman who will watch over my son is brimming with a mother's hormones.

MARTIN GOES FOR evaluations by physical, speech, and occupational therapists at the Santa Fe hospital's outpatient therapy department. The scheduling secretary notices me listening to the physical therapist's conversation with Martin and says, "You are overprotective."

I am furious. She knows none of my child's history and yet she is passing judgment on my mothering. But I fear that if I say anything to her, she may be harsh with him just to toughen him up. He will have to walk by her desk three times a week, so I say nothing.

The physical therapist, Sherri, understands Martin's goal—to regain the strength and stamina and skill to play once more on the Ultimate Frisbee team he joined last summer. He jokingly called it the "Big Boys' Team," to distinguish it from his friends who toss the disc around at another park. Because her husband plays on the Big Boys' Team, Sherri knows the level of recovery Martin wants.

On alternate days, Martin goes to another physical therapist, the woman who worked with me after our rollover accident last year. Her methods involve a great deal of stretching, and complement Sherri's dynamic routines.

And every day, Martin walks or jogs up the sandy arroyo he sometimes ran away to when he was a little boy.

THE SPEECH THERAPIST suggests that Martin take a course at St. John's College. She will work with him on any problems that come up. When I first call St. John's, they say they only accept full-time, degree-candidate students. Martin would be neither full-time nor a candidate for a degree.

Unwilling to give up, I call our neighbor, the St. John's director of admissions. His wife and I worked together on school projects when our children were younger. Larry asks the director of the St. John's Graduate Institute to meet with Martin. The Institute director admits him as a part-time, non-degree candidate, contrary to the college's policies. When I call to thank Larry, he says, "It helped that I knew Martin; that he wasn't a stranger. And the interview cinched it."

We have heard that Martin is more outgoing when we, his too talkative, too nosy family, are not close by. We ask him about the interview, but, as we expect, he has little to say. The director, Martin says, "was a nice guy. We had a good talk."

At the first seminar meeting, the students introduced themselves. Martin, when he came home after the seminar, said he had told the group that he grew up in Santa Fe and had studied at Harvard. Tom and I are surprised that he said nothing about his accident. It will be many months before we can do the same.

THE OCCUPATIONAL THERAPIST at the hospital declares that Martin is already, at their first meeting, better than most of her patients when she discharges them. She says he doesn't need OT.

But Martin thinks he needs more occupational therapy and calls Dr. Lakind. She suggests we call another OT, Chita.

We are becoming more confident in challenging accepted protocols. At New England Rehab, we learned that it's better not to wear hospital clothing while you're in the hospital, and that you can get bleach-free, rather than standard, sheets. We learned to get second and third opinions, finding a better rehab hospital than Spaulding, where most of the Mass General doctors and staff expected our son to go. Martin, too, learned to question authorities with confidence. At New England Rehab, he persuaded Dr. Suduikis to modify his liquid limitations and Dr. Ratner to decrease and finally discontinue his anti-anxiety drug.

When Chita comes to our house, Martin realizes that her son is an Ultimate Frisbee friend. Martin even drove him to the hospital when he was injured. In Santa Fe we say of this sort of connection, "small *pueblo*."

Chita is small and wiry, with white hair and dark eyes. She often does not finish a thought before the next one zips out of her. I sit at the dining table and take notes as she and Martin talk. When she pauses, I read back ideas she touched on but didn't say more about, so she won't lose track of any inspirations.

Chita recommends exercises that involve *crossing the brain's midline*, using left eye/right eye, left hand/right hand, near focus/far focus, and all their permutations, to run currents through the circuits in Martin's brain. She has him roll on the floor and, when the weather gets warmer, takes him outside to roll on the lawn. He rolls, with his eyes closed, trying to stay parallel to the wall he started from.

Twice a week Chita arrives at our house and dreams up new challenges.

Martin does every exercise she suggests. To improve his

coordination, he jumps around blue cones he's made by stapling construction paper to paper cups. He twirls on the trapeze we rigged in our big cottonwood tree for Sarah eighteen years ago. Dizzy, he steps off and works to regain his balance. He and Tom play catch and a variation of paddle ball, switching the paddle from the right hand to the left and back. They try patterns like *One Hit Right Handed; Two Left; Three Right; Four Left; Four Right; Three Left; Two Right; One Left.* Martin does better than Tom does, following the complex patterns they devise.

Chita says that learning a completely new musical instrument will be good for Martin's brain. A musician who gave him saxophone lessons nine years ago lends him a flute and becomes his teacher again.

DR. LAKIND TURNS out to be more than a supportive neurologist for Martin. She impresses Tom so much that I make an appointment with her for my mother. We have spent a year trying to identify the cause of Mother's unsteadiness, her frequent choking, and her weight loss. Two internists and an ear, nose, and throat specialist have not been able to help.

After ten minutes of talking with Mother and observing her, Dr. Lakind says she thinks that she has a form of Parkinson's. She orders tests to rule out other possibilities. Those tests done, she prescribes medications that cannot cure Mother, but that help her symptoms.

I take Mother to her many appointments. I am not surprised, after all I have learned about her, to see on Dr. Lakind's wall, beside her medical diploma, an earlier certificate from Columbia University, granting her a Ph.D. in philosophy.

She always asks after Martin.

I remember that when my father had his head injury, a friend warned that neurologists are inherently gloomy, because their patients' prospects are so bleak. It makes sense that Elizabeth Lakind, whose patients seldom get better, wants to hear about Martin's triumphs. I try to keep those conversations brief. I fear that every time Elizabeth and I talk about him, the unspoken message is that he matters more than my mother, who becomes smaller and weaker as the months go by.

IN MARTIN'S LAST days at New England Rehabilitation Hospital, the electro-diagnostician who discovered his tarsal tunnel syndrome called an orthopedist to look at him. Because Martin was in bed for the first weeks of his recovery, no one noticed what now is obvious when he stands naked. His left shoulder comes too far forward, and his left pectoral muscle seems almost concave. He looks as if he isn't standing as straight as he should. Something is out of place.

I remember Martin's EMT instructor. She told her students to look at the patient, not just at the machine. Martin's doctors might not have been able to see anything amiss until he stood up, but he stood up on his first Friday at New England Rehab. More than two weeks went by before anyone looked at him with his clothes off.

The orthopedist in Santa Fe confirms that Martin has a *posterior sternoclavicular dislocation*. The blow that broke his left scapula—his shoulder blade—in five places, has also dislocated his left clavicle—his collarbone—from its attachment to his sternum—his breastbone. The clavicle has healed in the wrong position, behind his sternum, and now may impinge on a major blood vessel, the brachycephalic vein. I wonder whether Martin's dislocated clavicle created the heart problems that alarmed the doctors who first saw him at Mass General.

The orthopedist refers Martin to a cardio-thoracic surgeon in Albuquerque, sixty miles away. I drive him to the doctor's office, and wait outside while they confer. Martin is disappointed that the specialist does not provide any helpful information.

Martin does research and finds a vascular specialist, also in Albuquerque. With Martin's arm in various positions, Dr. Jacob does Doppler imaging of the blood flow through his brachycephalic vein. He confirms that his clavicle impinges on his vein when his arm is in certain positions. Dr. Jacob's advice is simple: *Don't keep your left arm above your shoulder for more than brief moments, don't paint ceilings, and be careful when you sleep to avoid any position that makes your left arm tingle. Don't go rock climbing.*

Because the vein is close to the heart, surgery to correct the dislocation is dangerous. It would involve the *box of life*, that crucial area close to the heart that is filled with important blood vessels. Dr. Jacob says Martin can safely live with the condition, but because he has overcome so many challenges, it is hard for all of us to accept that this is one problem that can't be fixed.

In late spring, Martin goes rock climbing, even though the doctor has told him not to. He says he is careful not to get into positions where he has to keep his left arm raised for more than a few seconds. I am happy that he can still do the rock climbing that means so much to him, and I am uneasy too, whenever he goes off climbing with his friends.

Martin has traveled far on what Dr. Suduikis warned us would be a long plateau of recovery. He sees doctors on his own, drives alone, goes on solo runs, and devises challenges for his body and his brain. He is working harder than he has ever worked in his life. I trust his judgment, and I am beginning to be less afraid. As at New England Rehab, Martin's progress is faster than anyone has foreseen.

MORE AND MORE, it is Martin who evaluates his doctors. His training as an EMT, his ability to focus mentally, and his intuition—all combine to make him an astute patient. We ask him many questions, but defer to his judgment.

Martin discovers that an area in his field of vision is blurry. He has to move the page he is reading in order to bring words into focus. Once again it seems as though the doctors and the therapists did not look hard enough at the patient.

I drive him to Albuquerque again, this time to consult New Mexico's only neuro-ophthalmologist. The doctor declares, "The fourth cranial nerve on the right side of the brain has been damaged." He tells us the length of the nerve and the speed at which it grows. He predicts just how soon he will know whether the imperfection in the lower left vision quadrant has improved. When Martin returns a few months later, the doctor pronounces the nerve almost entirely repaired.

Martin sees an endocrinologist about his continuing thirst and his frequent sensation of needing to urinate. Returning with homeopathic medicines, he tells us that his difficulties are not serious and will ultimately resolve.

Our friends want to help. Martin considers every suggestion and tries many alternative therapies. He goes to one session with a craniosacral therapist, who manipulates his head in a way that Martin has asked the therapist not to. Martin immediately decides never to go back. I wish he would tell the man why he won't see him again, but he doesn't want to.

Friends come by. Sometimes they just want to see Martin and touch him.

ON ONE OF our drives to Albuquerque, I feel a sharp pain in my back, similar to a pain I had when I drove Tom to the Providence airport in mid-November. A urologist diagnoses kidney stones and orders lithotripsy. Shock waves will pulverize the stones into particles fine enough to pass from my kidney and out of my body.

I tell the anesthesiologist I am a cheap drunk, and ask him to use as little medication as possible. Then I start to cry. The nurse asks, "What's the matter?"

"It's our son," I sob. I cannot explain more than that. I know how thin the thread is that connects me to everything, everyone, I love.

A few weeks later I visit a Doctor of Oriental Medicine who has had some success helping patients with kidney stones. She talks about the correlation between emotions and the body's organs. The lungs, she says, have an emotional correspondence to grief, and the kidneys to fear. When the body is in balance, there is a healthy flow of energy, or *chi*, between the lungs and the kidneys.

"If the kidneys are weakened by fear or shock, they can't grasp the *chi* of the lungs. The lungs can't disperse the *chi* and they become stagnant," she explains. "There is nowhere for the grief to move. The grief stays buried." She goes further: "The strength of the kidneys is willpower, which can help you push through fear."

I have been on the edge, in a state of fear, for many weeks. My grief has not dissipated. My kidney pain began when Martin was in the hospital. My Doctor of Oriental Medicine, in helping my kidneys to function well again, is helping me move beyond my fear and face my grief.

Small Steps Back

Who shall ascend the hill of the Lord?

Psalm 24

MARTIN BEGINS TO put the rest of his life in order. Soon after our return to Santa Fe, a friend comes to eat supper with him. Tom and I go out. I would rather stay home with Martin, but he needs independence.

A few days later, on the afternoon of my early morning lithotripsy, Martin climbs nearby Monte Sol—Sun Mountain—with his friend. He comes home tired, hungry, and happy. I am in bed, in pain. While Tom makes supper, Martin sits on my bed and asks what he can do for me. We have switched roles, and he is caring for me.

On a sunny day when Sarah is home at Christmas, the four of us climb Atalaya peak, a mountain even higher than Monte Sol. Martin goes slowly. He stops often to rest and drink water. From the castle of rocks near Atalaya's summit, we look out over the city. We can hardly believe how high we have climbed, how far we have come. It is as if we own the world.

AFTER CHRISTMAS, MARTIN must decide whether to return to Harvard for the second semester, or wait to return until September. Although Tom and I worry about him trying too much too soon and want to care for him a while longer, we are concerned that we must not undermine his self-confidence. Martin talks about the pros and cons of returning soon versus waiting until the fall.

Tom worries more than I do that Martin needs to be with his college friends, particularly since most of his high school friends are no longer in Santa Fe. Tom wants him to be well enough to go back, to have this long nightmare over and done with. But, seeing that Martin is still weak, he agrees with me that it would be better for him to wait.

When Martin tells us that he has decided not to go back until September, we say only that we are sure he has made a thoughtful decision. We try not to let him see how relieved we are.

AT THE START of Harvard's semester break in late January, the three of us fly to Boston to move Martin's belongings from his college room into storage. We stay at Clint's, our second home. We visit Josefina in her home above the café, and go for tea with Dorothy and Diana, the Lowell House masters, in their quiet, elegant living room.

The city, with its noise and traffic and crowds, is too intense for Martin. As soon as we can, we leave for Cape Cod. A friend has lent us his house there. Dave and Rachel drive with us, and Sarah takes the bus from New York to the cape. We walk along the snowy beaches, watch videos, and play board games. We eat clam chowder at the pizza parlor.

Dave and Rachel have not seen Martin in two months. He was much weaker then and we, not knowing how much he would recover, were more frightened. Now, during our days together, we all play and laugh. When we rent *Cool Hand Luke*, our children discover that a number of Tom's favorite lines, lines they have grown up hearing, make a certain kind of sense. When the warden sentences Luke to a night in the wooden box, they recognize Tom's playful threat when someone, even, before he died, our dog, crosses him: "You're going to have to spend a night in the box."

I watch Rachel teasing Dave, lightly punching his arm. Martin seems not to have noticed. I remember Sarah's declaration last spring, when she first met Rachel, and think, *If she hurts Martin, I'll kill her.* A few months later, I tell Sarah how upset I was at Rachel's flirting with Dave. She says it's natural for a young woman to explore her newly discovered sexual power, and that she did the same at Rachel's age. She is twenty-three now, a BBC journalist, an adult.

Rachel leaves on Friday, Dave on Saturday. On Sunday, Tom drives Sarah, Martin, and me to Providence. While Tom and Martin watch football in our motel room, Sarah and I walk across the parking lot to a restaurant. As we wait for our take-out dinner in the bar, a moose head on the wall suddenly comes to life and sings, turning from side to side and blinking its eyes.

"Life is full of surprises," Sarah and I say together.

Early the next morning, she flies to New York and goes back to work. Tom, Martin, and I fly home to New Mexico.

From my notebook, February 21, 1999:

The sun is back where it was when you were injured, rising and setting at the same points on the horizon as it did on October 20. . . . Tonight I sat on your bed as you slept and touched your neck and your hair and your hands. Every day I give thanks for your presence, for your very being.

I am lost. I sleep for hours and wake feeling drugged. Am I being too patient with myself? It has been less than three months since we came home. How do I recover? This is— the kind of thing from which you don't recover.

Soon after he starts going to St. John's College in January, Martin comes home upset. A librarian at the public library got testy with him when he asked for help. I go to the library. I tell the librarian that he was impatient and unkind with a young man who is recovering from brain injury. The librarian acts impatient with me. I remember the hospital's secretary who called me overprotective. Martin is recovering. Am I?

From my notebook, February 26, 1999:

"This is the kind of pain from which you don't recover."

I found that line that has haunted me for months...

"But I'm still standing"—is the follow up I'd forgotten.

I am afraid to look at what happened, what almost happened, what can happen still in our lives, and I'm unwilling not to remember, know, and acknowledge.

Nothing is ever the same. Does the horror take away your faith? Does all the good restore it?

Why do I resent everyone who has not made an effort for us . . . who has not called?

. . . Is it those of us who have crossed a threshold—like Orpheus, and seen the Underworld, the world of no return?—who know how much we need the outstretched hand? . . .

Tom has visited his friend at the hospital twice, and called another to find out how his injured ankle is doing. He reaches out as he did not before . . .

Small steps back into the world. I'm still standing.

Letting Go:
Santa Fe, February 1999

who wants to look
like his mother sews his clothes,
wants to feel pinned
and gathered and snipped and sewed,
tucked and buttoned inside?

Wendy Mnookin, "Superman," <u>To Get Here</u>

IN LATE FEBRUARY, four months after the accident, Martin comes to me and says, "I want to get my own place."

I put my arms around him and say, "This is wonderful."

I start crying. He puts his arms around me and gives me tissues. He stays beside me for almost an hour and lets me cry. It is a bright clear day. The room is full of light.

Martin looks at places to rent. But none appeal to him.

ON MARCH 2, the brakes on a bus fail. The bus is filled

with sixth-graders coming down a steep, winding road from the Santa Fe ski basin. The bus crashes into a canyon wall. Children are bruised and broken. A boy who sat in the front seat is dead. As the driver struggled to control the bus, a father, Gary, stood up in the front and faced the children. He told them to put their heads between their legs, place their ski bags on top of their heads, and brace themselves. He may have saved many children, and he died in the crash.

His son, Tomás, has traumatic brain injury. I write a card to Cathy, Tomás's mother, Gary's widow. When I go to the hospital a few days later, she embraces me. She leads me into her son's room.

When Martin was hurt, Tom and I kept the vigil alone. Now, in Santa Fe, Tomás's uncles and aunts, grandparents, and his two young brothers crowd the room. The family, having lost their brother, son, father, husband, welcomes me into its center. I remember the Portuguese family that crowded the waiting room in Boston, the village gathered to heal someone they loved.

On a late winter day of another year, I will walk past the clothing store where Cathy worked before the crash and, on an impulse, go inside.

ALTHOUGH SHE DOES not work there any more, on this day Cathy is there.

We reassure each other that our sons are well. We sit on a sunny bench and tell each other stories.

Late one night, when Tomás had been in the hospital for several weeks, Cathy was alone with him, praying as he slept. She saw his head glowing. She shook herself to make sure she wasn't dreaming.

She knows that angels were healing Tomás.

AFTER GOING ON his own to look at places listed for rent in the newspaper, Martin asks if he can live in one side of the old adobe duplex we own. We had asked our tenants to move at the end of their lease, after Tom realized that the jammed lock and cracked door had been broken by our tenant, Michael, who had a nasty temper. Whenever we brought anyone to look at the house, Michael played angry music, filled the sink with something that smelled like rotten eggs, and scowled. We decided to wait to show the house until he and his timid girlfriend had left. Tom's assessment was, "He's a time bomb getting ready to explode."

A year later, the newspaper's police blotter will report that our tenant is in jail, charged with aggravated assault on and kidnapping of his girlfriend. We are sorry for her, and also relieved that Michael did not explode in our little house.

When the tenants have left and the house is empty, Martin tells us he wants to live there. We repaint the walls. We paint the dark ceiling beams and decking a pale cream. We buy a new stove and put new carpet in the bedroom. I sew muslin curtains and gather pans, dishes, towels, blankets, and sheets. Friends offer a futon, chairs, lamps, and a bedside table. Martin has his CDs and a player. My mother stopped driving when she moved to Santa Fe, and we give Martin her little Mazda. He surprises us by renting a small upright piano.

On a Saturday night, March 20, Tom and Martin and I shop for the kitchen items Martin still needs—a toaster and a spatula. We buy juice, eggs, toast, butter, and jam for breakfast. We toast his independence and health in his new house with a bottle of sparkling grape juice he added to our basket. It is five months since his injury.

AFTER MOVING ACROSS town, Martin often comes for supper with us. At least once a week I cook salmon, which Dr. Lakind says helps the healing brain. Sometimes, after exercising at a health club, Martin naps in his bed at our house before we eat.

Ryan, a friend since junior high, has come back to Santa Fe to have wrist surgery. He and Martin play left-handed Frisbee, Ryan because his right arm is in a cast and Martin because Chita emphasized that *crossing the midline* helps his brain repair itself.

OTHER NIGHTS, MARTIN cooks for Ryan or other old friends who still live nearby, or for new friends from St. John's College or the Hondo volunteer fire department. Martin had started volunteering at Hondo after high school, and had been a regular the summer after his first year in college, responding to pages on his radio, mostly for medical emergencies and occasionally for fires. The night before he flew to Boston after that summer, we had driven together late at night to return his radio and bunker gear—the firefighter's helmet, coat, pants, and boots. The station has no paid staff, only volunteers, and that night, no one was there. With Martin beside me in the dark, I sat in the driver's seat of the big red fire engine and learned to move the nozzle that shoots water at fires.

Now Martin goes to Hondo's department meetings and training sessions, and responds to fire and medical calls. He teaches us some firefighter terminology.

When he returns from a fire call one day, we ask, "Grass or structure fire?"

Martin answers, "That's an interesting question. Both."

What was burning was an unfinished structure that was being built out of straw bales, a new construction technique in Santa Fe. The next day's newspaper runs a photo of firefighters surrounding a smoking pile of straw. Martin stands in the foreground, wearing gear with reflective stripes and a yellow helmet, holding a red fire hose.

TOM AND I are eating supper when Martin comes in late one evening. He takes off his jacket, sits down, and asks, "Can I talk with you?"

He wants our full attention.

Leaving the weekly fire department meeting, he drove across the lonely country bridge over the interstate. In the dark, he sees a girl sitting above the highway on the railing. He drives back to the fire station. Others leaving the meeting also see her and return to the station.

They choose Martin, the youngest among them, to approach the girl.

They do not want to overwhelm her.

Martin walks to the bridge. He stops a good distance from the girl. He calls out to her, "Hey there, I'm Martin." The girl is crying.

Medics and firefighters wait at the far side of the bridge. The girl has been a resident at a nearby treatment center. A counselor from the center arrives and walks out to stand beside Martin. She speaks with the girl from that distance. Leaving the girl poised on the railing, she and Martin walk back to the other Hondo volunteers gathered at the edge of the bridge. The counselor says she fears that Laura may indeed jump. Someone must grab her.

Martin knows he isn't yet strong enough to wrestle her to the ground. He walks out onto the bridge with Charles. Charles, he doesn't have to remind us, is the paramedic who called in his own motor vehicle accident more than two years ago. Martin, then an EMT in training, drove Charles and his wife to the hospital in the ambulance.

Martin tells us his story slowly, with long pauses. Until he finishes, we cannot know whether he has been part of a tragedy or a rescue.

In the dark on the bridge, Martin speaks quietly to calm the girl. Suddenly, Charles runs, grabs her from the railing, and pins her to the ground. Other volunteers rush up, hold her down, and strap her to a gurney. They bring her to the hospital in the ambulance.

The next morning, I carry a letter to the hospital's psychiatric unit. I write the girl that Tom and Martin and I, people she does not even know, are praying for her to be well. I remember the note that came to Martin in New England. It said just that.

MARTIN THINKS ENOUGH time has passed for his left foot to recover from the tarsal tunnel syndrome Dr. Kassissieh detected in the New England Rehab basement. He has walked barefoot on the dry winter grass to stimulate his feet, but his left foot and leg still feel slow. He thinks that tap dancing will do more to challenge his foot than anything else. He calls several dancer friends to learn about teachers, and starts taking tap classes.

Six weeks later, in May, Martin dances in a tap recital. Katy and my mother drive with Tom and me to a saloon in the small town of Pecos, fifteen miles from Santa Fe. The walls are papered in red flocked wallpaper and the ceiling is low. All the dancers—middle-aged women, teenaged girls and boys, a fat young woman, and skinny Martin— perform in duos and trios and larger groups, twirling canes and bowler hats, elegantly tapping the saloon's oak floor. We all agree that the fat woman, so light on her feet, is the most unlikely dancer. Martin, with his long loose limbs and broad shoulders, is the most wonderful.

He comes to sit with us after his dance, and Katy and I wipe away our happy tears before he can see them.

SARAH SAYS WE need a family vacation. In June, Tom and Martin and I fly to Los Angeles to meet her. We drive north along the coast to a misty village. At our simple motel we read and play shuffleboard in the light rain.

We tour the Hearst Castle. Tom, at the back of the group, keeps slipping into rooms the guide has passed by. My naughty husband keeps me on edge, but, as always, he does not get caught.

We drive south to Long Beach for a night on the Queen Mary, where years ago Martin made the magician his straight man on the Grand Ballroom stage. We wander below decks through exhibits of the ship as a World War II troop carrier. Wax figures of soldiers play cards and sleep on bunks stacked three high. My father was one of the soldiers who crossed the Atlantic on the Queen Mary. I tell Sarah and Martin that their grandfather is the figure in the corner, the man writing in a little notebook while other soldiers play cards or sleep.

We take a small boat to Catalina Island, where Tom and I hiked and camped the spring I became pregnant with Sarah. Halfway to the island, we see churning water. The turbulence moves toward us and we are surrounded by more than a hundred dolphins. The captain slows the boat, and on either side, ahead, and behind, dolphins cruise just under the water, and then explode into air. We are dazzled in a dancing sea.

A Room of His Own

"Calling All Angels"

Eliza Gilkyson, Song Title

ELEVEN MONTHS AGO, not knowing whether Martin would live, not knowing whether he would learn to walk again, and not knowing what faculties could be saved, nurses, doctors, and therapists did everything they could for him. This is what they do every day, and they don't get much good news.

I send New England Rehab Hospital a large print of the newspaper photo of Martin in his firefighter's garb, holding the hose to fight the straw-bale house fire.

In the fall, when he is ready to go back to college, Tom and I fly with Martin to Boston.

WE WANT TO visit New England Rehab. I call ahead to make sure it isn't Dr. Suduikis's day off—not that she often takes a break. When we come up to the top floor of the hospital, Sue, the physical therapist, is waiting in the sunny atrium, many months pregnant.

Martin tells her he has regained the full range of motion in his arms.

Sue challenges, "So, are you going to show me?"

He sweeps his arms in circles and she beams. Her toughness, when she told him she would have him sitting upright within a week, was a front. Sue was mothering Martin all along.

We do not stay long at the hospital. It feels to me almost as if we have gone to visit our old kindergarten, and that, although everything is familiar and friendly, the chairs are too small.

We don't belong here anymore.

MARTIN HAS NOT let the matter of his sternoclavicular dislocation go. He has made an appointment with a doctor at Mass General, who, according to his research, is the single best expert to consult about the dislocation.

I wait in the outer office while they talk.

Dr. Leffert confirms that nothing can be done. The dislocation cannot be fixed. He tells Martin not to hold his left arm above his shoulder for more than a short time. Martin has followed every lead to learn what to do about his dislocation. Now he accepts what cannot be changed.

I realize that we are on the tenth floor of Mass General, near both the neurological ward and the Neurological ICU. I want to find Lynette DiAngelo, the ward nurse who awed us with her competence and speed. Martin cautions me that he has no memory of that time. He won't recognize her.

The ward nurses tell us Lynette now works in the Neurological ICU. We walk past the bank of elevators Tom and I stood by so often, and pass the waiting room where we sat with our friends and with relatives of others inside the ICU. We come at last to the ICU.

The receptionist sees me through the window in the locked door. A year ago I was so focused on getting to Martin every time I rang the bell, I barely noticed her, but she remembers me and buzzes us in. She has never even seen Martin, who never left his bed.

Lynette is not on duty today. The receptionist calls out, "Does anyone remember Martin? He was here a year ago."

His nurse from his first afternoon in the ICU comes to the receptionist's desk. Annie is Snow White lovely, with black hair, fair skin, and dark blue eyes. She has only ever seen Martin lying down, and now, as I introduce them, she looks up at him. Annie is one of the nurses Tom and I imagined would be a neurosurgeon if she'd been born male and middle class, but now she is just a young woman looking up at a strong young man.

After we leave, Martin asks if all the nurses were beautiful. "Annie was the fairest of them all," I say, "and they were all beautiful."

IN KURT VONNEGUT'S *Slaughterhouse Five*, there is a scene where Billy Pilgrim's father tosses Billy, then a small child, into a swimming pool, shouting, "Sink or swim, Billy." Billy lies at the bottom, not moving, hearing the careless laughter above him.

We remember Harvard as a place where, if you couldn't swim,

you sank. Tom was 3000 miles from California, where he'd lived since his father's death six years before. When he finished high school, his mother moved to Japan to teach. He stayed in the dorm at Thanksgiving. At Christmas, he spent a few days in New York with cousins he hardly knew, but most of those winter weeks he lived alone in the locked and cold dormitory—Harvard had turned the heat down—climbing the fire escape and crawling through the window to his room.

I fared better than Tom, but I knew some who sank—a girl from Montana, a boy from Houston, and others, like them, far from family and home. Harvard has become more compassionate since then. It runs several programs that bring incoming students together before classes begin. Two years ago, Martin spent a week with other freshmen, hiking in the New Hampshire mountains, camping by a lake, and shivering in the relentless rain. Teenagers who didn't know anyone in their class made friends before they had to meet their assigned roommates, choose courses, and start studying. If students couldn't swim, the college wanted to help them stay afloat.

Gene McAfee, Lowell House's senior tutor, tells us about Harvard's Office for Student Disabilities and its Bureau for Study Counsel. He says they can help Martin with any difficulties he runs into. He encourages him to take a reduced course load, and says, "If the load still seems too intense, drop a course or even two." He will help with whatever Martin needs.

The Lowell House secretary finds a rare "single" for Martin, a tiny sitting room with a desk, a tinier bedroom, and a bathroom. He won't need to ask a roommate to be quiet when he needs to rest.

From his second floor window, we see the church tower clock

across from the Café Pamplona. Josefina's basement café has hardly changed since Tom arrived in Cambridge thirty-five years ago.

Tom's older brothers had both worked in the café before Tom started college. Josefina offered a warm place he could visit, and, eventually, a place he could stay during vacation breaks when the college closed down.

When I took Sarah and, later, Martin east to look at colleges, we stayed on the top floor above the café, crawling into our narrow beds under Josefina's eaves. Now almost 82, Josefina still runs the café. We bring her flowers and she feeds us, an exchange that's lasted over thirty years. I hope she will become a haven for our son.

IN SMALL WAYS, the accident alters Martin's college path. His first semester back, he decides to take three rather than the standard four classes. Inspired by his activities *drawing on the right side of the brain*, which Chita prompted, and taking her advice to try new things for which he may have no particular aptitude, he takes a drawing class. He is content when he gets a C for the course.

From my letter to Diana and Dorothy, Lowell House Masters, after Martin's return:

> *It is incredibly hard being away from Martin. We kid that*
> *he moved out to live on his own in March to wean me from*
> *caring for him, and it's true I may have needed toughening*
> *up more than he. Knowing that he was well enough to live*
> *separately and was getting stronger steadily more than*
> *counterbalanced my missing him. But sometimes, between*

two appointments on our side of town, he took a nap at home in his bed in his room, and I rejoiced.

THE CRIMSON RAN a front page story and photo about the accident the morning after it happened. They printed updates on Martin's condition for weeks. In October, almost a year after the accident, a *Crimson* reporter e-mails me, asking me to call her. She wants to do a follow-up story.

I call Martin. Sarah is visiting him, and they have been talking about the reporter's request. Like me, she initially thinks the idea interesting.

Sarah and Martin talk about how easy it is for a reporter to get things wrong, if only small things. He is certain the *Crimson* reporter cannot possibly get everything right—the facts, maybe, but not the nuances. He decides that the only way to avoid a misleading story that might upset him is not to have any story at all.

Martin forwards to me the reporter's e-mail to him:

. . . I want to stress that the focus of the article will be the astounding task of physically recovering from a serious accident such as yours. How can one even begin to cope with such a life-shattering event in a context where most of us get tremendously upset if we get a bad grade or are passed over for a fellowship?

. . . your story is pretty inspirational and students deserve to hear about it, especially since some of them may be wondering what's happened since the accident. . . .

He also sends me his reply:

> *Thank you for your concern and interest. I am flattered by The Crimson's desire to do a story about my recovery. However, I simply do not want the publicity. Thank you for your understanding and tact.*

Martin has the sense to get advice from his sister, the journalist, and he has found a graceful way to protect his privacy. He can take care of himself.

Farewells and Celebrations:
Massachusetts, September 1999

A generation goes, and a generation comes,
but the earth remains for ever.

Ecclesiastes

TOM AND I HELPED MARTIN move his belongings back from Maggie and Bill's house where we had stored them in January. We slept at Clint's and made forays to visit Tom's mother, taking her on drives and out for lunches while Bill was at work.

On trips to Boston since our blowup two years ago, we have had one supper together with Maggie, Bill, and Bill's girlfriend, Connie. Still, despite our strained relations with Bill and our awkwardness with his fretful and tense girlfriend, we hope that Sarah and Martin can create their own relationship with their uncle. They must make arrangements with him to see their grandmother, who is 93 and no longer the independent woman she was when I first met Maggie more than thirty years ago.

They want to go to Uncle Bill and Grandma Maggie's for

Thanksgiving. They know Bill says we don't give him enough notice of our plans and that, no matter when we plan a trip east, it is never a good time for him. They ask if we think inviting themselves three weeks before Thanksgiving is too short notice. Hoping Bill will be more flexible with them than he is with us, we encourage them to call him.

Bill welcomes Sarah and Martin and, after some hesitation, their friend Erin. Erin has been a family legend since she told her foul-mouthed classmate, "You could be so much more eloquent."

After high school, Erin studied fashion design in Paris. She gets on well with Connie, who is a Francophile as well as an artist. Maggie isn't sure who Sarah and Martin are, but she enjoys having company and is cheerful and friendly. Martin always calls her "Grandmother" to help her figure out who he is.

That afternoon, Grandma Maggie says to Sarah, "I don't know what to do anymore. I feel as if I've done it all."

TWO WEEKS LATER, Bill telephones. Maggie fell in the kitchen that morning and broke her femur. I listen to Tom talk with Bill and think, *This may be the beginning of the end of Maggie's long life.*

After Maggie's surgery at nearby Mount Auburn Hospital, the doctors want to send her for rehabilitation. Partly on Tom's recommendation, Maggie goes to New England Rehab, where Martin was so well treated. A month later, they find gangrene in her leg.

Maggie goes back to Mount Auburn Hospital on January 10. She gets antibiotics to battle the infections in her bloodstream.

Bill is in a state of panic.

Tom flies to Boston. Henry, the middle brother, comes too

and stays with Bill. Tom stays at Clint's and goes to meet his brothers early each morning. Together, they consult doctors and look at nursing homes.

At the end of January, Maggie is moved to a nursing home in Lexington, north of Boston. Tom puts bright posters on the walls of her room and hangs a mobile of painted wooden fish. He reads to her from an old book of nursery rhymes. Sometimes she joins in, reciting from memory.

After three weeks, Tom returns to Santa Fe. The infection in Maggie's blood grows stronger. The brothers talk every day. Tom reassures Bill that Bill is doing everything that can be done. We both think that not much—beyond keeping Maggie comfortable—can be done. Bill says that Maggie is too young to die.

NOT LONG BEFORE his dementia took over, my father had said he wanted to lie in a plain pine box and rest. It was five and a half years before he got his wish.

I think, *Maggie does not know one day from another. What would more time mean to her?* I hope that she will have an easy end. To me, now seems as good a time as any.

Maggie becomes so weak that the nursing home sends her back to Mount Auburn Hospital. Bill calls the next afternoon. The nurses have told him Maggie will die within hours. Tom and I debate whether to call Martin. We consider how he will react to what is happening. We wonder whether, with his own death so recently averted, we should call him at all.

We realize we cannot decide for him. Martin will decide what to do.

He goes to Mount Auburn Hospital immediately. Bill is short-tempered and angry with the nurse. The nurse is unpleasant and angry back. I imagine the hostility was nastier than what happened the morning over two years ago when Tom and Bill fought and I went upstairs to pack our suitcases. Then, Bill was being challenged about how he cared for his mother. Now his world, with her as its center, is ending.

Martin speaks first to Bill and then to the nurse. He tells each of them to speak only to him. He will be the messenger for everything between them.

The youngest by decades, he knows what is needed and creates peace. The discord in the room dissolves and Maggie dies. Martin closes his grandmother's eyes.

MARTIN ASSESSED THE situation and took charge. Tom wonders whether *he* would have realized, as Martin immediately did, that creating a peaceful space, where she could let go, was the only priority.

I remember how, when I fell and fractured my skull, Martin stayed at my head, the person who, according to medical protocol, was in charge. I wonder if his EMT training has also taught him how to assess a crisis fast. Did it teach him the importance of taking control when others are not up to the challenge?

Perhaps his early rebelliousness was rooted in his uncommon independence and imagination. He has found ways of coming at challenges from unexpected angles, particularly since his accident. His skill in finding paths around obstacles helped Maggie when she was dying.

We remember how, after his accident, Martin said, "I was in absolutely top physical and mental shape when this happened, and I will do whatever it takes to get back to where I was."

Tom and I think he is in top emotional and spiritual shape now.

TOM AND HIS brothers want to bury Maggie's ashes next to their father's grave. In March, we fly to Chicago, the city Maggie grew up in, a city Tom barely knew as a child. We stay in a hotel beside Lake Michigan, midway between the Art Institute I love and the Field Museum of Natural History, where Tom could happily spend a week. We look at paintings in the Art Institute the first day and wander the Field Museum the next.

Sarah flies in from New York and Martin from Boston. It is dark when we bring them to our room. We pretend that it is nothing special, and watch their awe when they walk in. We have left the lamps turned off and curtains open. Along the shore of the lake, lights stretch as far as we can see.

Walking to supper, we pass a flower shop, closed for the night. In the morning, we go back and buy tulips and daffodils, sunflowers and daisies—*marguerites*, for Grandma Maggie, Margaret. We drive north to the cemetery where Tom and Henry and Bill's father was buried forty-two years ago.

The cemetery worker sets the box of Maggie's ashes into a hole he has already dug and steps away. We stand in a circle, bundled up against the cold. Although Bill and Henry have said they do not want any ceremony, Tom does. He says what a brave adventurer his mother was. When she was fifty-two, after their father died, she left Chicago, where she was born, went to college, married, and raised her three boys. She made a new life for herself not once but three times: first in San Diego, where she moved after her husband died; then, when Tom had finished high school, in Japan, where she taught for two years; and, finally, outside Boston, where she lived until her death.

I go next, reciting an inscription from the Field Museum's Egyptian tomb.

Martin reads from the *Tao Te Ching*, an ancient text he likes.

Sarah tries, but cannot speak for tears.

To our surprise, Bill and Henry also speak.

Henry echoes much of what Tom has said about their mother's courage and high spirits.

Bill says he is angry that his mother's death came sooner than it should have. Then he tells something he has hidden at least for all the years I have known him. He has been angry with his mother for years, because, when he was nineteen, she did not let him help care for his dying father. He is glad he got to show her that he could care for her.

I am astonished to hear Bill admit an anger that may be at the root of how he has treated Maggie. I see a man who has seemed locked away from any feelings other than anger and resentment, and I hear him talk about wanting to be the caring son his mother would not let him be so many years ago when his father was dying.

We pass flowers to Bill, Henry, and Connie. We all set them on the grass beside the box of Maggie's ashes. Sarah lays her last flower on the grave of the grandfather she never knew.

AFTER LUNCH, WE drive to Grove Street, where the brothers grew up. A new house has been built on half of the double lot that was theirs. We stand across from their old house on its now small lot, and the men point out their bedroom windows. Sarah walks across the street and rings the doorbell. The woman who answers says the house has been renovated and is not at all the same. She does not invite us in.

After the others leave for the airport, Tom walks Sarah, Martin, and me around the corner, to the house where his childhood friend, Joanne, lived. Tom tells our children a story, one I have heard before. He had been ill and missed a few days of school. When he was better, he rang Joanne's doorbell. Her father came to the door. Joanne had died. As Tom tells his story to our children, I hear again his bewilderment at the mystery of death.

We drive into the village. Tom rode his bike along this street. He says, "I would pedal, pedal, pedal, pedal, pedal." He takes us into the library and shows where he checked out books, and then, "Pedal, pedal, pedal," he drives us to the train station where his father took the train into Chicago to work. We drive east again, "Pedal, pedal, pedal, pedal," to the shore of the lake. We walk out on the jetty, take off our shoes, and dip our feet in cold Lake Michigan.

CHICAGO'S NAVY PIER has been converted into an amusement park and convention center, an urban cluster of restaurants and boutiques. On this cold March day, it is home to a spring festival. We walk through a Japanese landscape and tulip gardens, breathe in roses, hyacinths, and daffodils, and wonder at the many trees none of us can name.

When she last visited us, Maggie wanted to garden all day. When we didn't have enough projects to keep her busy, Tom gave her a cushion to kneel on and set her to weeding the grass that grew into our gravel driveway. She was happy.

They have trucked tons of dirt onto the pier for the garden show. The air smells green and alive. How happy Maggie would be to see us exploring a garden on the very day we set her in the earth.

ALMOST A YEAR later, we gather in Maggie's house that now is Bill and Connie's. Henry has come from Washington, D.C., Sarah from New York, and Martin just up Massachusetts Avenue from Cambridge. Maggie's sons will divvy up her possessions, a third to each.

Although Maggie's bedroom is the house's largest and has the best light, Bill and Connie have not moved into it. The green and red quilt we gave Maggie one Christmas still covers her bed. Her clothes still hang in the closet.

But Bill surprises us once again. He asks Sarah to come to Maggie's bedroom and gives her, his mother's only female descendant, the wedding band and ruby ring that Maggie always wore. Perhaps Bill will move on.

WHEN HE RETURNED to Harvard, Martin joined Kuumba, a group that sings African and African-American music. After the winter concert, someone told him that a woman in the audience asked her son, "Who is that skinny white boy in the back row who looks as if he's having more fun than anybody else?"

We go to Kuumba's spring concert with Clint and Josefina. The concert is in Sanders, a theater in Memorial Hall, a brick architectural curiosity built to honor Harvard's Civil War dead. Over thirty years ago, I sat in Sanders twice a week in a class on *The Legal Process*. Tom and I went there one fall morning in Martin's first semester to sit in on his *Moral Reasoning* course.

No matter how compelling the performance it houses, Sanders Theater stuns me with its own majesty. The oak seats rise in a semicircle around the great wooden stage. The ceiling and the balcony's underside are also oak. I feel as if I am inside the Ark, in a space God might have designed.

Kuumba performs on Martin's twenty-second birthday. Watching my skinny white boy in the back row, I grip Josefina's hand and cry through the spirituals.

Tom and I have come to Cambridge after a short holiday. One evening in a Savannah bar, a trophy fish on a plaque suddenly began to sing. Although *Big Mouth Billy Bass* became a cliché, with numerous spin-offs, back then no one had ever seen such a thing. It was a perfect gift for Clint. We went to several stores before we finally found a singing fish to buy.

We give a party for Martin at Clint's. Clint is still at work in his downtown Boston office when I cook dinner. Tom attaches *Billy Bass* on his fancy plaque to the rough-sawn wood wall beside the wood stove, below the deer's head and next to an old-fashioned fishing creel. *Billy Bass* looks like just another trophy on the wall.

When Clint comes home, Martin's friends are sitting by the cozy woodstove, along with Dave's visiting father and younger sister and brother.

Clint downs a couple of vodkas in the kitchen before he joins us.

After a while, Dave's father notices the deer on the wall.

"Did you shoot that deer?" he asks.

"Yes," Clint says, "but I never went hunting again. That's Bambi."

"And the fish?" Dave's father asks.

"What fish?"

"That one there, below Bambi, next to your fishing creel."

"Never seen it before in my life."

"Right," says Dave's wary dad, "and I suppose you don't know what the plaque says either."

"Can't say I do," says Clint.

I am sitting on the ottoman beside the woodstove. Tom asks me, "Can you read what the plaque says?"

I go to the trophy wall. Leaning over as if to steady myself as I read, I push the button that starts Big Mouth Billy Bass singing, *Don't Worry, Be Happy*, moving his head and wagging his tail in time to the beat. Everyone laughs until their sides ache. Clint laughs most of all.

Six months later, the fish is selling for a quarter of what we paid, but the night it sings for Clint, when no one has ever seen a singing fish with a dancing tail, it is worth a fortune.

Company in the Dark

We help each other through the blind
Tall night beneath the infinite spaces. . . .

Archibald MacLeish, "Creator"

ALMOST FORGOTTEN IMAGES surface, and I wonder how they fit into what I am piecing together.

1962, the day after Thanksgiving, Princeton

I am fourteen. The big poodle's toenails click across the floor. Lauren has gone to answer the phone, and her house feels too quiet, the room too big. She comes back with news. Our classmate, Buff, has died in a plane crash. She and I spent the afternoon together just two days ago. I call my father to drive me home. He holds me in the crisp, cold night and says, "This is something you will never understand." We are an island of two in a dark universe.

His words comfort me for years. They tell me that my father is beside me, company in the dark.

1982, Santa Fe

When my father loses his mind, I am lost. I look to Tom to rescue me. I can't see that he is lost too. Every morning I wake crying, picturing Daddy tied to his bed so he can't hurt himself. I don't understand that Tom is giving the only comfort he can give, just being beside me. I hold on to the notion that someone can make everything all right.

1998, Boston and Santa Fe

Many people wrote that they were keeping Martin and us in their thoughts. Others wrote that they were praying for us. One friend sent a watercolor she painted at Santuario de Chimayó of the church and its walled garden. The nurses asked about the small bag of reddish dirt our friend sent with her painting. It was healing earth, we said, gathered from *Santuario*, a shrine in a mountain village north of Santa Fe. Pilgrims pray for healing there, and offer thanks for recovery.

Another friend went to the Santa Fe cathedral, sat by the statue of Mary holding Jesus, and lit a candle. She tells me that, over twenty years ago, when I went east with my baby after my father's accident, she fasted for a week, praying for my father all the while. We had been friends for only a few months, and she had not met Daddy.

Sarah's friend who stayed in our house when we went east, listened to messages that came to our house while Martin was in the hospital. She says that, when she witnessed his incredible recovery, she learned how powerful prayer can be.

A card to Martin from a friend whose adopted daughter is from Mexico:

> *Flor has been very worried about you and has even gone to the church next door to pray for you. She tells me that you have an angel on your shoulder who is watching over you. She says she knows this because she has one too.*

I used to think there was a difference between those who prayed and those who didn't. Now I think that there are people who say *pray* and others who call it something else.

Apollo 13

Necessity is the mother of invention.

Old Proverb

SARAH, OUR FIRST BORN, was often the one on center stage. She made us laugh when, a small child, she demanded we all shush at the dinner table. "I'm the talker," she said.

After prom in her junior year—which began with Emily's date locking his keys in the car and ended with the girls wishing their dates had danced with them more—Sarah and her friends decided they could do better. Six girls resolved to go "stag" to their senior prom. They curled their hair and pressed on fake fingernails in our bathroom, squeezed into shiny dresses in Sarah's room, and went to dinner together at a fancy restaurant. A woman quizzed some of them in the ladies' room and, when the group of teenaged girls rose to leave for the prom, the restaurant, which had been buzzing with their story, broke into applause.

SARAH GOT HER first job, an internship at the BBC, only

198

after a disastrous interview. Early in the day, she rode the subway half asleep from Columbia to her downtown interview. In England, she later learned, anyone hoping for the internship would thoroughly research the BBC and, on the morning of the interview, prepare by reading the day's newspapers.

When her interviewers asked what stories she thought would make good subjects for them to cover that day, Sarah had nothing. She left the BBC office appalled at her poor performance.

She was thrilled by the intelligence and wit of the two men who had interviewed her. As she drank her first cup of coffee of the day, she wrote them a letter acknowledging her poor performance, asking for a trial internship, and promising to disappear forever if, after two weeks, they did not want her. She got her two weeks' trial, worked there as an intern for three college semesters, and, two and a half years later, when the car hit Martin, was producing and reporting for the New York Business Bureau of the BBC.

A star and a producer in her life as well as at work, Sarah, when Martin is hurt, becomes a supporting player, shining the spotlight on him. Now she says, "He's my hero."

TOM, WHO DOES not easily show his feelings, transforms his anger and impatience into perseverance, pushing to get the ventilator out, the sedative reduced, our questions answered. Always eager to get going, he sits by Martin hour after hour, telling him he loves him, battling with him over water, willing him to get well. The first time Martin stands, wailing at the pain of being upright, Tom cries out how proud he is and how much he loves Martin.

Whereas I revisit painful memories in order to conquer them, Tom tries not to awaken them. Then one day he tells me he has talked with a friend about Martin's injury and about my father's similar injury more than twenty years earlier. Echoing his friend, he says, "Perhaps Martin was given the chance at life your father did not get."

Although still wary of magical thinking, Tom is looking at the world with new eyes.

AS FOR ME, I have found stamina I did not know I possessed, strength to keep on doing what needs to be done. And I worry less.

When the children were small, I had a theory that dangers should be rated on both likelihood and seriousness. The first person crossing the stream calls out that the rock is wobbly—not serious, but likely. Even on slow back roads in the forest, you don't let children ride in the back of a pickup because it could bump them out—not likely, but serious.

Now, when either of my children is out late, I sleep better than I did before. I learned that bad news travels fast. I think, *My children are fine, or I would have heard.*

All my years imagining catastrophes made me no more ready to cope in a crisis. They only wore me down.

THERE ARE OTHER changes. I look at the moon differently now. When the car hit Martin, the moon was new and the night dark. His jacket was black, his jeans navy blue, and his shirt a dark plaid.

I still make a wish at the new moon, as my superstition-loving English mother taught me to do, but now I like watching it grow, having it stay in the night sky longer, giving light to guide us home.

I do not walk where I used to. I stay off streets and walk up the arroyo instead.

Before, when I saw people pushing wheelchairs, I felt awkward, uncertain how to react. Now I see an ache in each caretaker. I remember Martin wondering why the cafeteria cashier asked him was he a patient. I couldn't bear to tell him he walked crooked. I didn't want him to wonder who was watching him.

Walking out of a market with bags of food for Martin's birthday dinner, I notice a man pushing shopping carts up the ramp. I can see that his mind is slow. I remember Martin saying, "I was in absolutely top physical and mental shape when this happened and I will do whatever it takes to get back to where I was." I begin to cry.

The muddled man selling newspapers in the middle of the street was once someone's darling boy. Now he sells papers by the stop sign, wearing an orange safety vest.

But my son seems more than ever himself, without self-consciousness or apology. His radiance in the presence of those who love him awes me.

HOW FINE IS Martin? He has always been slow and thoughtful. In one college application essay, he wrote:

> Recently, I've been making connections in my head.
> Connections between subjects. In every class, I learn about

one particular subject. That's all we do in class; there's no
time for anything else. Everything is neat and carefully
packaged. I move from a block of calculus, to a block of art
history, to a block of music. All these blocks are supposed to
stack nicely in my brain. There is only one problem: my
brain isn't a cube.

Martin still resists neat and careful packaging. He listens to others' ideas and opinions, and finds his own path. Sometimes I wonder if he is slower than before, but he has always been slow to respond, thoughtful and contemplative. Sometimes exasperating.

As a child, I learned to wait for my father's answers just as I often wait for Martin's. Unlike my speedy mother, and unlike Sarah, Tom, and me, Daddy was slow and discerning. He gave everything the thought it deserved. Daddy's slowness was central to his wisdom. Martin is much like him.

Is it harder now for Martin to do several things at once, to wipe the counters while he talks? He never liked to divide his energy, and now he often chooses to go slowly, and to do one thing at a time. Yet he is the best driver in the family, with good judgment and quick reflexes. And when he's in Santa Fe, he works as an emergency medical technician, where fast responses are vital.

Trying to sort out how Martin may have changed is like trying to stack blocks when I should be tossing flowers in the air.

From my letter to Sarah, after Martin went back to Harvard and I visited her in New York:

That year it came as a great surprise how many
sad things could happen at once. At first you

202

might think the odds are that one grief might exempt you, but that year I learned the odds are that nothing can keep you safe. So many concurrent painful events altered our sense of each one, just as a color appears to change when another color is placed beside it.

(Francine Prose, "Talking Dog," The Peaceable Kingdom)

Dear Sarah,

. . . I know I talked about how important it was to me to have gone back: to the ICU, to New England Rehab, to visit Dorothy and Diana, to the same bed I slept in at Clint's . . . to spend some time with Martin's friends. To be in all those places and with those same people, and to have Martin well, in some way undid the spell of my sorrow.

I remember so well lying in your bed last year, holding you and saying how happy I was at that very moment. And then the phone rang [with the news that Martin was injured]. Funny, I had not thought that being with you there was something I needed to revisit, but it must have been, because in many ways being with you in New York was a final step in the return to life I was seeking.

. . . . Francine Prose's excerpt . . . seemed an important acknowledgment of my frame of mind. . . . The question Francine inspires in me is, Knowing that nothing can keep us safe, how do we live? . . . I watch Martin in the way that he has of being absolutely present in his joy at being with those

*he loves, and I feel as though, knowing that nothing can keep
any of us safe, he knows how to live.*

IN THE MOVIE *Apollo 13*, there's a scene when the astronauts are stranded on the far side of the moon. The troubleshooters in Houston's Mission Control dump duct tape and wire and hoses and empty boxes onto a table, making a pile of everything in the spaceship. Their task, using nothing but what is on the table, is to invent a way to bring the astronauts safely home.

When Martin is hurt, everything we have—Sarah's energy and independence, my anxiousness and compulsive note-taking, Tom's impatience and his many questions, Martin's stubbornness and his crazy-making slowness—is there in the pile in front of us.

We just need to find new uses for a few old parts.

Some of our obstacles suggest new paths. When the hospital's occupational therapist says she can't help, we find Chita. When we can't rent our little house with the ticking time bomb tenant, we make a safe place for Martin to live.

After a small stroke, my mother keeps forgetting to wear her emergency call necklace and refuses the walker that helps keep her balance. I tell Martin my worries, and he says, "You know *you* can't keep her safe." His words help me. If I can't solve every problem, I can at least accept uncertainty as a given in my life.

We work with what we are given. Tom and Sarah and I cannot rescue one another. No longer looking for rescue, I find them beside me, sharing the journey.

I keep climbing out of fears that beset me, learning to take things as they come.

I AM DREADING the accident's first anniversary, Martin, back at Harvard, calls to say he is hosting a party that evening. He celebrates his survival. So do we.

Havana, Cuba, 2000

El dolor es la sal de la vida. [Sorrow is the salt of life.]

Fernando Velazquez Vigil, 2001 art exhibit in Havana, Cuba

THE FALL OF 1998, Harvard University was negotiating with the U.S. Treasury Department for a license so they could sponsor students and professors traveling to Cuba. Martin had plans to meet with a professor from the University of Havana. He wanted to study there so he could learn about Cuban music first-hand. Then he was hurt.

In the January break after his first semester back at college, Martin flies to Havana with other Harvard students for a literature seminar at Casa de las Americas. He meets with administrators there and at the University of Havana, and tells them he wants to come back as a regular student the next fall.

Martin needs to submit vast amounts of paperwork for his semester in Havana: Harvard's Treasury Department license; a letter from the Center for Latin American Studies confirming that he is under their auspices; Harvard's pre-approval of credit for courses; his passport; his transcript; letters of recommendation from his Harvard professors, from the director of Casa de las Americas, and from a professor of the Havana seminar. Martin must request, receive, copy, and fax them all.

When he arrives in Havana, Martin finds a room to rent less than a mile from the University. He e-mails us:

> *The place I am staying in is very nice. High ceilings, good light, independent kitchen, baño, and entrance! The owner lives in the same building, just through a door that we keep closed and locks from both sides. She is a very nice and helpful woman.*

He enrolls in three classes: Latin American Literature, Latin American Art, and Afro-Caribbean Studies. He finds a Spanish-language tutor to help him prepare his papers and oral presentations. The only other American undergraduates at the University of Havana are enrolled in a special program their colleges arranged. They live together in a mansion in Miramar, a neighborhood that was elegant in the years before the Revolution.

After a month, the University administration office tells Martin he must move to a student dormitory across the bay, a forty-five minute bus trip from the University. They either mistrust an American undergraduate living on his own or, perhaps, they just want him to pay room and board to the government-run dormitory.

Martin gives up his *very nice* place and moves across the bay.

Many months later, he tells us that he was not formally accepted as a student until he had moved to the dormitory, several weeks after the term began. We are troubled that he put himself into such an uncertain situation without telling us. We also recognize how much his self-confidence has recovered since his accident.

Because it is so far to travel from the university back to the dormitory, he also secretly rents a modest room in Centro Havana, close to the University. He stays there more often than in the dormitory. If his New England Rehab OT could see him shopping in the open air *mercado*, cooking on a two-burner stove, washing his dishes, his laundry, and himself, in cold water, and making do in a culture where making do is almost an art form, how she would praise his mastery of the *activities of daily living*.

WITH MARTIN SETTLED in Cuba, Tom and I decide to take my mother to England. She often talks about old friends she wants to see again. She wants once more to sit and look over the soft green hills of Sussex and Kent, to watch sheep graze on the Downs, where her family picnicked when she was a little girl.

Sarah has been working in London since March. Since she first worked at the BBC as an intern four years ago, she has gone from simply coming up with ideas for stories to producing features and even voicing a few reports. Still proving herself to the London higher-ups, she works the dusk-to-dawn shift. When morning comes, she goes home to sleep. In the afternoons she will have a few daylight hours to spend with us before heading back to work.

When we arrive at the flat we have rented, Sarah has stocked it with bread and butter and jam, eggs, milk, sugar, tea, and coffee. She won't let me reimburse her. She is an adult, welcoming her family to her world.

It's a cold and rainy September. Tom keeps lending his rain jacket to my mother. When she was younger, Mother would never have come to England without a raincoat, but now she hasn't planned ahead—and I haven't realized how much I need to take over. I buy myself a new raincoat so she will wear the one I brought and Tom can keep his jacket.

One afternoon, I see she is limping. We settle her on a bench and I take off her shoes. All her toes are red, and one is bleeding. She has not noticed anything wrong and suddenly is in great pain. I buy her new shoes, but she won't throw the old too tight ones away. I don't realize that Mother's stubbornness is not just her usual obstinacy, but an early symptom of dementia.

We have sweet times too. We go to tea with her friend from the war. Norma, like Mother, now is smaller and thinner than before. She arranges pillows to make Mother's chair softer, walks her to the bathroom, and strokes her bony hand. Her husband and I watch them in silence, bystanders to an ancient friendship.

When I go upstairs to the bathroom, I stop by the bedroom door. In the stark room there are no rugs on the dull wood floor. Two narrow beds are tidily made up, each with a gray blanket and one thin pillow. Downstairs, the table is laden with tea party treats.

Back in our carpeted modern flat, Mother takes a bath in the shiny, deep tub. She calls me to help her out. She is wet and slippery, and I cannot lift her. I sit on the toilet seat while we consider our options. She gets the giggles. We call Tom to lift her out of the bathtub. I hold a towel to wrap her in, just as I used to wrap Sarah and Martin after their baths.

Getting into her seat on the airplane heading home, Mother

bangs her leg. There is no spare flesh on her, and she bruises easily. We hold an icepack on her shin across the Atlantic. Despite her protests, we arrange for a wheelchair when we land. Pushing her, we are sent to the front of every line. We pass through immigration and customs in a few minutes. We determine always to travel with an old lady in a wheelchair.

The next day, October first, her six-month London stint finished, Sarah flies home to New York.

Subj: *a serious and important message*
Date: 11/8/2000 1:24:01 Mountain Standard Time

Dear mom, dad, and sarah:

This e-mail relates a somewhat grave event that happened to me. Before going on, I want to emphasize that I am doing fine now and there is no need to worry. I do not want you to worry but I need to tell you because I love you and know that you love me.

On Monday afternoon I was assaulted. It was one of those freak events, broad daylight in a country where this sort of thing does not happen. None of my Cuban friends, nor the administrators at the University can believe it.

Four men approached me from behind and I was unaware. One of them got me in a choke-hold and I was unable to breathe, much less yell for help. I struggled and landed some blows as well as received some. However the choke-hold was tight and I lost consciousness from lack of breath. When I came to, I was on the pavement and my *aggressors were trying to pull my back pack off me but I was somehow tangled in the straps. I started to yell for help and they took off running. Within a matter of moments a group of concerned Cubans was gathered around me. This all happened on a street that runs along one side of the university at about 4:50 pm on Monday afternoon. Again, no one can believe that it happened in an area of the university either. But when I got up with the help of some of these concerned Cubans, I walked with them to my facultad (probably 100 meters and around a corner). There, I encountered some of the program group of N. Americans. One of them, Glenn, took me just up the hill to the emergency room of one of Havana's main hospitals. I was attended to well, had a couple of x-rays of my jaw which were all clear.*

I have one friend, Ivon, who is a nurse in the neurosurgery ward at this same hospital and by good luck she had just come on shift. The docs wanted me to be assessed by a neuro-doc anyway because I told them of my past history of severe head injury. Ivon also already knew of my history. I stayed the night in the ward where Ivon works for observation, and in the morning went for a C.T. Scan of my head (in another building of the same hospital).

I have been well cared for. One of the chief administrators of the university came to the hospital to check on me and asked to be kept informed. I spent last night at the mansion of the Americans, who were all very concerned. They brought me dinner and I rested (they also brought me updates on the election coverage; better than baseball! As of the moment I still do not know who won. At last report it was down to a recount in Florida. Fluck Forida. The reports were favoring Bush, Uuugh. . . . Fader may have nucked us.)

Today, I have a minor head-ache (day after a concussion) and some minor bruising to the side of my face and jaw. Taking Ibuprofen. But I feel better and physically I am fine. The emotional side of all this has not been easy. Frightening and unexpected. I called my close friend Meiladis, from the E.R. and she came immediately. That helped. As did having Ivon around. And Ivon's boyfriend, Nigel, Canadian and a good friend of mine, by good fortune stopped by to talk with Ivon. He stayed with me a while and that was really nice.

So I'm on the other side of this unfortunate and freak occurrence and the sun is shining (literally and metaphorically). The only thing my aggressors were able to take from me were my Cuban I.D. card (the administradora of the Univ. said she would make me a new one) and my sunglasses. They were clearly trying to rob me because they spotted me as a foreigner—nothing more, the violence was a means to that end. That day I was carrying my larger and flashy looking backpack to haul some stuff around. I am careful and I will be more careful. Please be concerned for me but do not worry.

You can call me . . . tomorrow morning at around 10 a.m. my time (8 yours). I will wait until 10:30 for your call. I have tried to provide you with details in this message so that we do not have to play 20 questions on the phone. Of course you will have more questions, which is fine. There was no charge for the care I received at the hospital. God love this aspect of socialism.

    I love you, and love you, my family.

    Martin

As I read the e-mail, it is hard for me to breathe.

Tom is out somewhere. I have learned a little about waiting and know it will be better for him to read the letter when he comes home than for me to call him now. I telephone Martin's neurologist and forward his e-mail to her. Dr. Lakind wants him to have some more tests. She and I agree that he sounds calm and coherent, with his humor, and his penchant for spoonerisms, intact.

The next morning Tom and I call Havana. Aware that Martin does not like talking with both of us on the telephone together because of how our conversation jumps around, we have planned out what we will say and ask.

We ask as few questions as we can. All three of us are frightened, and we all work to sound calm. Tom and I ask Martin to have the medical tests that Dr. Lakind advised. He says he will e-mail her to discuss them.

Two days later, he sends another long e-mail, about his Latin American Literature midterm exam, exams coming up in *Arte LatinoAmericano* and *Estudios AfroCaribeños*, going to a film with a friend, and the *cute girls/women* in his *facultad.* He continues:

    I gave my friend Nigel your name and phone number and told him to watch for any changes in manner/personality. . . . I think this incident in a way threw us all back to October-November of 1998. I could hear not only the scare in your voices when we talked over the phone but also something like that mode you learned of dealing with all the papers and procedures from 1998. And understandably so (some of my first thoughts after being injured recently were about my past injury and recovery). However, I can say with certainty that there will be other times in my life when I will get hurt and we all cannot go back mentally to 1998 every time I get a scrape. I imagine that both of you were already aware at some level of what I just said. I have no easy solution. Poco a poco, como dicen. Talking about it and bringing it into the open may be one of these steps. . . .

I SAVE MARTIN'S e-mail to read again later, and go outside. What else can I do?

I see trees and clouds and sky, and I hear ravens calling.

I breathe in air that smells of leaves and earth.

Poco a poco, 2002 and Beyond

His very near death and miraculous recovery from serious brain injury after being struck by a car on Memorial Drive . . . drove home once again the frailties of our human state and bodies as much as the amazing subconscious will and ability of youth to survive and bloom.

Traver Clinton Smith, Jr., "Harvard 35th Anniversary Report"

MARTIN WROTE HIS SENIOR THESIS on Cuban salsa music for Harvard's department of Folklore and Mythology. He came home to Santa Fe a few months after he graduated.

As he anticipated, there have been other times in his life when he got hurt. He called us late one night to say he'd fallen asleep on the highway driving home after working as a deejay in Albuquerque. When we got to him, his old Honda was wrecked. We held each other in the clear, cold night, told the tow truck driver to unload the wreck in Martin's driveway, and drove home together.

THERE WILL BE other times. We cannot go back every

time. No easy solution.

SIX YEARS AFTER our trip to England, my mother was tired of living. She had fallen too many times, her wounds wouldn't heal, and she was sick of the pain and the drama. As she wished, she died at home—in the library that for many years had been Martin's bedroom. I slept beside her, and Martin and I sang to her.

When she died, I brushed her fine hair into a white halo and walked out into the snow as they took her body away. It was Sarah's birthday—a fearsome symmetry.

Tom and I gave up restoring old houses soon after Martin's accident, but in time we took on a big project. We bought six run-down little houses on two neglected acres. We had lived in the smallest casita when we first came to Santa Fe.

Now we're finding uses for some old parts we stashed away years ago. We're almost done with renovating bathrooms and replacing old windows, and now spend most of our time planting trees and seeding hardy native grass where burrs and stickers used to grow.

After more than thirteen years in New York, Sarah moved back to Santa Fe. She struggles to balance her work, which she mostly loves and which could take every minute of her time, with a non-work life that is full with a kind husband, a child, many friends, Martin, Tom, and me.

Martin left his job as a paramedic and firefighter a few years after my mother's death. He keeps his passion for Cuban music alive, working as a deejay, and going to concerts and dances. He travels as an audio-visual technician to cities in Europe, Central America, and Asia.

Much of that work is troubleshooting—if there weren't unforeseen problems, he says, he wouldn't be needed. He became a wilderness medicine instructor. He still plays Ultimate Frisbee and rock climbs. A couple of summers ago, he took up kayaking, and, when he's mastered that, he'll find another challenge.

Zachary, our grandson, has his own red rake and blue shovel. He likes flowers, bees, leaves, and dirt. He pretends to play the violin and the saxophone. He loves garbage trucks, trains, and fire fighters. He plays Fire Chief Zach, rescuing stuffed animals from danger. Sometimes I call him Martin by mistake.

Martin's injury and recovery are no longer at the center of my world. We see him when he comes for supper and when he comes by our house to play with Zacky. He helps me with my computer, and I sew buttons on his shirts. We talk politics, books, and movies. He invites us to supper and parties at his house.

MARTIN WOULD RATHER I not say too much more about his life. As he told the college reporter who wanted to do a follow-up story about his recovery, he simply does not want the publicity.

ACKNOWLEDGMENTS

I have named only a few of the quiet heroes we met during this journey. Paramedics, nurses, nursing aides, doctors, therapists, and caring friends—thanks to you all. I am especially grateful to Dr. Joseph Ratner for his kindness and encouragement.

Joan Anyon, Harvey Mudd, Carol Oppenheimer, Emilie Osborn, John Osborn, Warren Perkins, Katy Power, Morty Simon, my husband, my daughter, and my son all read my manuscript early on, and their questions and criticisms made this a better book. Richard Mahler, an old friend, has been a superb editor. Louise Klingel Casselman designed my fine cover.

Clint, your loyalty and generosity have made you the godfather we needed for our son, the friend we rely on.

Some readers wondered where I "found" my epigraphs. All the poems I used have been with me a long time. I have counted on poetry, just as Martin counts on music. When I was ten, a woman visited our class, crouched on her chair, closed her eyes, and spoke Carl Sandberg's "Fog." That magic woman, Moyne Smith, taught me in high school, passing on her passion for poetry.

I have worked as a poetry editor—mostly a matter of telling what doesn't work and being ready to say *Yes!* when it does. I have taught English—reading poems I love to my students, going for goose bumps whenever possible. When my son was in the hospital, Theodore Roethke's poem, "In a Dark Time," sustained me.

PERMISSIONS